John McLaren McBryde

A Study of Cowley's Davideis

John McLaren McBryde

A Study of Cowley's Davideis

ISBN/EAN: 9783337180034

Printed in Europe, USA, Canada, Australia, Japan

Cover: Foto ©Thomas Meinert / pixelio.de

More available books at **www.hansebooks.com**

A STUDY OF COWLEY'S DAVIDEIS

A DISSERTATION

PRESENTED TO THE BOARD OF UNIVERSITY STUDIES OF THE
JOHNS HOPKINS UNIVERSITY FOR THE DEGREE
OF DOCTOR OF PHILOSOPHY

BY

JOHN McLAREN McBRYDE, Jr.

PROFESSOR OF ENGLISH LANGUAGE AND LITERATURE AT HOLLINS
INSTITUTE, VA.
FORMERLY FELLOW IN ENGLISH AT JOHNS HOPKINS UNIVERSITY

[REPRINTED FROM THE JOURNAL OF GERMANIC PHILOLOGY, VOL. II, No. 4.]

TO

MY COLLEAGUES AND FORMER FELLOW-STUDENTS,

FREDERICK TUPPER, JR.

AND

JAMES PINCKNEY KINARD.

TABLE OF CONTENTS.

A STUDY OF COWLEY'S DAVIDEIS.

THE literary reputation of Cowley has undergone many vicissitudes. In his own day accounted superior to Milton and to Tasso, he is now almost completely forgotten, and even of his most enthusiastic admirers very few can be found who have read through the *Davideis*, the subject of the following investigation. For this neglect the poet can blame no one but himself. He had a loftiness of purpose and a seriousness of thought far in advance of the other poets of his school; yet he had not the strength to resist the popular taste, nor the judgment to select only the enduring qualities of his age. (Compare Dryden's well-known simile of the drag-net.) Dr. Grosart has eloquently defended Cowley against the 'elaborate and weighty' criticism of Dr. Johnson, and against Mr. Gosse with his 'smoky or jaundice-yellow pair of spectacles,' and has catalogued in detail the *enduring* poems, passages, and lines of Cowley. It is not the purpose of the following study to enter into a criticism of the poet. Very few, however, will dissent from Dr. Grosart's thesis, that Cowley has been too much neglected in our day, and that both as a lyrist and a prose writer he has made some notable and lasting contributions to our literature. It was as an epic writer that his failure was most conspicuous, and his *Davideis* has justly sunk into oblivion, in spite of Rymer's judgment in pronouncing it superior to Tasso's *Jerusalem Delivered*. The purpose, then, in resurrecting this almost forgotten epic of Cowley's is not to make it a basis for a criticism of the poet, but to show in some slight way the growth of the religious epic prior to Milton, and the part which Cowley took in its development.

BIOGRAPHICAL SKETCH.

Abraham Cowley was the 'posthumous son of Thomas Cowley, citizen and stationer, and of the parish of St. Michael Le Querne.'[1]

As his father's will was dated London, Parish of St. Michael le Querne, July 24, 1618, and as the poet died July 28, 1667, in his 49th year, Dr. Grosart places the approximate date of Abraham's birth between August and December 1618.

Cowley was entered at Westminster School as King's Scholar, the exact date of his admission not being known, and here at the age of ten years he wrote his first poem, an epical romance, entitled *The Tragicall Historie of Piramus and Thisbe*, and dedicated to Mr. Lambert Osbolston, Headmaster of Westminster. Two years later he wrote another little epic, *Constantia and Philetus*, and in 1633 his poems were collected into a volume and published with the title *Poetical Blossoms*, and with a dedication to the famous John Williams, Bishop of Lincoln, at that time Dean of Westminster. These schoolboy efforts were well received and went through several editions, so that the young writer, being tempted to try with his muse a still more lofty flight, wrote, while still at Westminster, his first drama, a pastoral comedy in English, entitled *Love's Riddle*. This was published in 1638, with a dedication to Sir Kenelm Digby.

Leaving Westminster then, with a reputation as a rising man of letters, he entered Trinity College, Cambridge, where he took the oath June 14, 1637, and was admitted as Westminster scholar (Lumby, *Prose Works*). In the same year Richard Crashaw was elected Fellow of Peterhouse from Pembroke Hall, and from this time dates the friendship between the two poets. It was at this period, too, that Cowley began his *Davideis*, and that Crashaw probably made his translation of the first book of Marini's *Strage degli Innocenti*.

[1] Peter Cunningham, *Johnson's Lives of the Poets*, 3 vols. 8vo. 1854 (Murray), I, 3, quoted by Dr. Grosart, I, x. See also J. L. Chester, *Notes and Queries*, 4th Series, XI, 340.

In 1639 Cowley received his Bachelor's degree, and October 30, 1640, became Minor Fellow. According to Lumby he was not admitted as Major Fellow, and probably left Cambridge without proceeding to a full degree. Dr. Grosart, however, on the authority of the *Alumni Westmonasteriensis*, gives among the landmarks of Cowley's progress at Trinity :

> Chosen a Major Fellow in 1642.
> Proceeded M.A. of Cambridge in due course.

And Anthony à Wood (*Fasti Oxon.* II. col. 209, note) has the following entry: 'Abraham Cowley, admissus Socius Minor Collegii Trinitatis Oct. 30, 1640. Major (Socius) Mar. 16, 1642. Reg. Coll. Trin. Cant.' Still further proof of the fact that Cowley finally proceeded to his M.A. is seen in the following letter of Vice-Chancellor Ferne re-instating the poet in his fellowship (quoted in full by Lumby, p. XVII) :

'Whereas we received a letter from his Ma'ty dated the last of January in behalf of Mr. Abraham Cowley, Fellow of Trinity College, for the continuance of his seven years before taking holy orders, in regard of his being elected immediately after his taking degree of Master of Ars, etc.,

H. FERNE.'

Wood also states that Cowley was M.A. of Cambridge.

At Cambridge Cowley's literary activity continued. He contributed a Latin poem to the Συνῳδία *sive Musarum Cantabrigensium Concentus*, a collection of verses upon the birth of Princess Anne (March 17, 1636/7), so that from the outset his sympathy with the royal party was strong. Among other distinguished contributors to this collection were Thomas Chambers, the Vice-Chancellor, Samuel Collins, the Provost of King's College, James Duport, afterwards Bishop of Peterborough, and Richard Crashaw. Cowley wrote various other Latin poems, and on the 2d of February, 1638, a Latin comedy of his, entitled *Naufragium Joculare*, in the style of Plautus, was performed by the men of his college before the members of the University. It was printed the same year, with a dedication to Dr. Comber, Dean of Carlisle, and Master of Trinity.

When on the 12th of March, 1641, the King passed through Cambridge with his little son Charles (afterwards Charles II), an entertainment was hastily arranged for his benefit, and Cowley wrote for the occasion his comedy *The Guardian.* It was not printed till 1650, though meantime it had been acted privately 'during the troubles.'

In February 1643/4 came the commission of the Earl of Manchester 'to take special care that the solemn league and Covenant be tendered and taken in the University of Cambridge,' and as a consequence Cowley, in common with nearly all the Masters and Fellows, was forcibly ejected from the University. Together with Crashaw and many others, he took refuge in Oxford, then quite a Royalist stronghold, and entered St. John's College. Here he became intimate with Lord Falkland, to whom he afterwards addressed some lines. He attached himself to the Royal cause and secured an introduction to Baron Jermyn, afterwards Earl of St. Albans, one of the Queen's most trusted friends and admirers. Through him Cowley was brought into her service, and when in July 1644 the Queen escaped from England and took refuge in Paris, Cowley accompanied her as secretary to Lord Jermyn. His duties as secretary were arduous, and his life in Paris was distasteful to him ; yet he managed to continue his literary work, and wrote while there his collection of love poems entitled *The Mistress.* In Paris he met his friend Crashaw again, then in actual need, and introduced him to the Queen. Through her, Crashaw was appointed secretary to Cardinal Palotta, and died in Italy a short time later, soon after he had been appointed one of the Canons of the church of Loretto.

In 1656 Lord Jermyn sent Cowley to England, in order that he might, says Sprat, 'under pretence of privacy and retirement, take occasion of giving notice of the posture of things in this nation.' Shortly after reaching his native land, he was seized by mistake for another, but as soon as his identity was discovered he was cast into prison.

While in prison, in 1656, he published the first collected edition of his poems in folio, containing *The Miscellanies, The Mistress, Pindarique Odes*, and *Davideis*.

Through the influence of his friends he secured his liberty this same year, and Sir Charles Scarborough went his bail for the sum of £1,000. In the following year, in September 1657, Cowley acted as groomsman at the marriage of the Duke of Buckingham, and wrote a sonnet upon the occasion.

December 2d, 1657 (Wood, *F. O.* II, col. 209), he secured the degree of M.D. from the University of Oxford, and withdrew into Kent, where he devoted himself to the study of botany, in order, says Sprat, ' to dissemble the main intention of his coming over.' As a result of his study, he wrote his *Plantarum Libri*, published in 1662, and included in his *Poemata Latina* of 1668.

' Taking the opportunity of the confusion that followed upon Cromwell's death,' says Sprat, ' he ventured back into France, and there remained in the same station as before, till near the time of the King's return.' Of this, his second sojourn in France, we have no account.

In 1660 he returned to England and published his long and labored *Ode upon his Blessed Majesty's Restoration and Return*. On the 11th of February of this year he was restored to his Fellowship at Cambridge (Lumby).

The following year he wrote his famous *Discourse by way of a Vision concerning his late pretended Highness, Cromwell the Wicked*, and his *Proposition for the Advancement of Experimental Philosophy*.

Cowley's efforts to obtain from the Government substantial aid in recognition of his long and arduous services, all ended in disappointment. An absurd charge of treason was brought against him, and Charles II had nothing to give him but posthumous praise. The Mastership of Savoy had been promised him by both Charles I and Charles II, but he never received the appointment. It was at this gloomy period of his life that he wrote his *Complaint*, styling himself the 'Melancholy Cowley,' for which he was ridiculed in some verses beginning 'Savoy-missing Cowley has come into Court,' wrongly attributed by Mr. Leslie Stephen to Suckling (*Dict. Nat. Biog.* 'Cowley ').

He then retired from public life to Barn Elms, on the banks of the Thames, and through the influence of his friends, the Duke of Buckingham and the Earl of St. Albans, secured a lease of the Queen's lands.

Thus relieved from want, he continued his literary work. In 1663 appeared his *Verses upon Several Occasions*. In this same year, the Royal Society was founded, and Cowley was one of the charter members. He took great interest in the science of the day and wrote, about this time, his *Ode to Mr. Hobbs*.

In April 1665, he removed to the Porch House in Chertsey. There, in spite of his troubles with his tenants and neighbors, he continued his literary work. During these last years of his life, he wrote his *Essays*, and only a few months before his death, he composed his *Ode to the Royal Society*.

He died July 18, 1667, in the 49th year of his age, and was buried in Westminster Abbey, near Chaucer and Spenser.

THE FAMILIAR LETTERS OF COWLEY.

Bishop Sprat, Cowley's friend and biographer, to whom the poet bequeathed his private papers, refused to allow the familiar letters in his possession to be published, and set forth in his biography his old-fashioned views in regard to the matter. As a consequence he has drawn down upon his head maledictions of all sorts. 'What literary man,' says Coleridge, 'has not regretted the prudery of Sprat in refusing to let Cowley appear in his slippers and dressing-gown?' and this regret has since been voiced by every reader and every editor of Cowley. Mary Russell Mitford, in her *Recollections of a Literary Life*, 1, 65, goes so far in her resentment as to call the innocently offending Dean a ' Goth and a Vandal.' It has been assumed that all of Cowley's familiar letters were lost or destroyed. Dr. Grosart, in his Memorial Introduction, regrets that 'utterly disproportionate search and research have aided very slightly to the biographical data. Specifically I have been more than disappointed that none of the mass of his "familiar letters" which Sprat certainly possessed, has been traced. I cannot believe that he destroyed them.'

It seems almost incredible that ·such a careful and painstaking editor as Dr. Grosart should so completely have overlooked two articles in *Fraser's Magazine* (Vols. XIII, 395; XIV, 234) containing several apparently genuine copies of these much-sought-for familiar letters of Cowley. They are easily accessible to the general reader by reference to Poole's Index (1882) under the name 'Cowley',[1] yet it is remarkable that no editor or biographer of the poet has called attention to these letters.

The articles in *Fraser*, which are unsigned, are entitled 'The familiar Letters of Cowley, with notices of his Life and Sketches of some of his Friends and Contemporaries —Now first printed.' The writer of these articles thus explains how these letters came into his possession (*Fraser* XIII, 397): 'We are now by a most fortunate circumstance enabled to state that a large portion of these letters is preserved, and has been placed in our hands for arrangement and publication, by a descendant of Dr. Sprat. Of their authenticity proofs can be afforded which will satisfy even the incredulity of Mr. Disraeli, by whom we are certain the discovery will be hailed with delight in his forth-coming "History of Literature."'

The first article opens with a brief but admirable criticism of Cowley and of the metaphysical school, in which the editor proves himself a man of wide learning and

---

[1] In *Notes and Queries*, 8th series, VIII, 465, Mr. Roberts refers to this apparently forgotten article on Cowley in *Fraser* XIII, and regrets that such a 'vast area of valuable information in the better class of periodicals of the earlier part of this century, is practically a sealed book to literary inquirers.' In *N. and Q.*, 8th s., IX, 51, a reply was made to Mr. Roberts, in which it was suggested that *Poole's Index* is just such a general index as is required.

good judgment. Then follows the first letter, 'To his Mother, after her sickness, with Consolations for Mourners,' dated Trinity College, March 3 (year not given), and signed 'Your affectionate son, A. Cowley.'

The second letter is ' To Mr. William Hervey, with an account of a visit to Ben Jonson, a Sketch of Cartwright, and a Notice of the Sad Shepherd.' It is signed 'A. Cowley,' but has no date or place attached.

In vol. XIV of *Fraser* is printed one more letter, addressed to 'My beloved friend, C. E.', dated Trin. Coll., May 8, 1637, and signed 'A. C.'

The editor's heading is, 'Anacreon at Cambridge. Lyric Poetry. Pindar and Sappho. With a notice of the Davideis.'

Here, then, was apparently a noteworthy find,—no less than three of the 'familiar letters' of Cowley, so highly praised by Dean Sprat, and so eagerly sought for by recent students and editors of Cowley. If genuine, they would be of almost priceless value, worthy to be placed beside the famous Conversations of William Drummond of Hawthornden with Ben Jonson.

Several considerations, however, awaken the suspicion of the careful student. Towards the close of the first letter, ' To his Mother after her Sickness,' there is a reference to Herbert, ' Hear what holy Mr. George Herbert says,' and here follows the last verse of *The Flower*. Moreover, the editor himself refers to a letter written by George Herbert to his mother after her sickness, and dated Trinity College, May 29, 1622. A comparison of the two letters reveals a verbal correspondence too close to be accidental. In the so-called Cowley letter we read: 'For consider, dear Madam, that we never read in the Scriptures, " *blessed be the mighty*, or *blessed be the wealthy*, but blessed be the poor, and blessed be the mourners, *for they shall be comforted*" ' (*Fraser*, XIII, 400). Herbert offers consolation to his mother with exactly the same words from Scripture : ' But, O God ! how easily is that answered when we consider that the blessings in the Holy

Scripture are never given to the rich but the poor! I never find "Blessed be the rich," or "Blessed be the noble," but "Blessed be the meek," and "Blessed be the poor," and "Blessed be the mourners, for they shall be comforted"' (Given in Walton's *Life of George Herbert—* see also Grosart, *Herbert's Works, Fuller Worthies*, London, 1874, III, 491 ff.).

Again in *Fraser*, p. 400, a few lines further on, we read, 'and in another place, "Casting all your care upon Him, for He careth for you,"' with which compare Herbert's letter (Grosart, III, 493-494), 'And above all, if any care of future things molest you, remember those admirable words of the Psalmist, "Cast thy care on the Lord, and He shall nourish thee" (Psal. LV). To which joyn that of St. Peter, "Casting all your care upon the Lord, for He careth for you" (I Peter V, 7).'

This similarity is not mere coincidence, and yet how could young Cowley have had access to Herbert's private letters written fifteen years before, and not published by Walton till 1670?

The description of Ben Jonson given in the letter to Mr. William Hervey is clearly based upon Aubrey, to whom indeed the editor refers: 'Cowley's description of the poet accords with the few particulars we possess concerning him. The studying chair and the loose horseman's coat are mentioned by Aubrey, who derived his information from Lacy, a well-known comic actor of that day, and intimately acquainted with Jonson. The credulous antiquary adds that the chair was such as Aulus Gellius is drawn in' (*Fraser*, XIII, 403).

Cowley's description is as follows: 'He is now confined entirely to his apartments, rarely wandering further than from his bed to his studying chair, which is of straw, and covered with a cloth wrapper such as the old country wives use. We found him wrapped in a large and loose great coat, with slits under the arms, like those we have often seen at Newmarket. His face, once, as I have been told, very fair and beautiful, is now roughened, as it were, by a scorbutic eruption, to which he has long been subject. His eyes are rather grave and thoughtful than bright, and one seemed to me somewhat bigger than the other.'

Compare Aubrey (Clarendon Press ed. 1898, II, 12 ff.) ' He was (or rather had been) of a clear and faire skin ; his habit was very plaine. I have heard Mr. Lacy, the player, say that he was wont to wear a coate like a coachman's coate, with slitts under the arme-pitts. . . . I have seen his studyeing chaire, which was of strawe, such as old women used, and as Aulus Gellius is drawen in.' On p. 14 of Clark's *Aubrey* is to be found the note about Jonson's eyes, which, suggests the editor, 'may come from that " Chronicle of the stage," as reported to Aubrey by John Lacy.'

' B. Jonson ; one eye lower than t'other and bigger.' ' Ben Jonson had one eie lower than t'other, and bigger, like Clun, the player.'

The conversation of Ben Jonson in this letter is obviously based upon Drummond of Hawthornden's conversation with Ben Jonson, as even the most casual reader would note at a glance.

' Our conversation turned upon the Muses,' the Cowley letter has it, 'and he spoke, as his custom is, with great admiration of Donne, repeating from the " Calm " two lines, which he said were admirably descriptive of unbroken stillness :

> " In the same place lay
> Feathers and dust—to-day and yesterday." '

In a foot-note, the editor of the letters calls attention to the fact that Drummond of Hawthornden has printed these verses incorrectly ; clearly a blind to mislead the unwary reader.

Compare *Conversations with William Drummond*, Shakespeare Society, London, 1842, p. 8.

' Cowley.' ' " My friend Donne," he said, " will perish through the ignorance of his readers ; his oracles require an interpreter." '

Conversations, p. 15. 'That Donne himself for not being understood, would perish.'

'Cowley.' 'after all, Daniel was nothing but a verser.'

Conversations, p. 2. 'Samuel Daniel was a good, honest man, but no poet.'

So much for the internal evidence. At the conclusion of the second article (*Fraser*, vol. XIV), the editor enters upon a criticism of the *Davideis*, and closes with a promise to produce more letters containing 'Interesting notices of Cowley's reappearance in London.' But here all trace of the letters disappears. More remarkable still, in the contemporary literature of that period there is absolutely no reference to these letters, even though the editor boldly says that they would be hailed with delight by Mr. Disraeli in his forthcoming *History of Literature*. In the *Amenities*, however, published in 1840, no mention is made of this treasure trove.

Equally puzzling was the fact that not one of the recent editors and critics of Cowley had taken note of these so-called 'Familiar letters' in *Fraser*. To resolve my doubts I addressed a letter to Mr. Leslie Stephen, Dr. Richard Garnett, of The British Museum, and Rev. A. B. Grosart, stating the facts of the case and requesting an expression of opinion. They were unanimous in agreeing with my first supposition that the letters were but clever forgeries.

The question then arose, what could have been the motive for foisting these supposititious letters upon the public? Dr. Garnett of the British Museum I have to thank, not only for his kind reply to my letter of inquiry, but also for the suggestion of the authorship of these 'Cowley Letters.' One has to take only a brief glance at the majority of articles in *Fraser* (vols. XIII and XIV) to discover their real character. In the January number for instance, the first sixty-two pages are devoted to a mock Parliament of the *Fraserians*, in which the principal speakers are Oliver Yorke, Mr. T. Moore, Mr. E. L. Bulwer, Mr. Alaric Attila Watts, The Ghost of Goethe, Dr.

Southey, Mr. T. Carlyle, Mr. Lockhart, The Ghost of Coleridge, Sir Edgerton Brydges, Mr. Wordsworth, Sir Walter Scott, etc., etc. In fact, from this wonderful Parliament Mr. Kendrick Bangs might have easily obtained many hints for his *Houseboat on the Styx*. In this article appears very prominently the name of *Father Prout*—F. S. Mahony — a name intimately associated with *Fraser's Magazine* between the years 1834 and 1836 inclusive.

Francis Sylvester Mahony (1804–1866), the Bohemian Scholar priest, was born at Cork in Ireland, in 1804. His life, full of pathos and romantic adventures, is sympathetically portrayed by Mr. Charles Kent, Barrister-at-law.[1] Having pursued his early education in the Jesuit College of St. Acheul, at Amiens, and in the Jesuit Parisian Seminary in the Rue de Sèvres, where he became marvelously skilled in the Latin and Greek languages, he removed to Rome in order to complete his studies in the Jesuit College there. Here his health gave way, and he was forced to return to his native land, before attaining the great desire of his life, ordination to the priesthood. His four-months' experience as Master of Rhetoric at Clongowes Wood College, with John Sheehan, the Irish Whiskey Drinker and others of that stamp, reads like a chapter from one of Samuel Lever's rollicking romances. He returned to the Continent after his unfortunate escapade with the convivial Irish youngsters, and in Rome, after long and persistent endeavors on his part, and resolute opposition on the part of the Jesuit Fathers, he was finally ordained priest. He never felt in full sympathy with his profession, however, and gradually drifted away from even the customary practices of religion. Literature was a more congenial occupation, and he became a contributor to various magazines and periodicals of the day. His connection with *Fraser's*, extending over a period of two years, began with the publication of *Father Prout's Apology for Lent*, in which he recorded his Death, Obsequies,

---

[1] See *The works of Father Prout*, ed. by Charles Kent, London, 1881, Biographical Introduction.

and an Elegy, April 1834. From this date appeared every month *Reliques of Father Prout*, published from his posthumous papers. The remainder of his life is the story of a Bohemian journalist, of his wanderings over the European Continent, settling for short periods at Rome, at Paris, and at London. It was in Paris that he spent the closing years of his life, and it was there, reconciled to the church, and comforted with the consolations of religion, that he breathed his last, May 18, 1866.

During the period 1834–1836, Francis Mahony was one of the most brilliant contributors to *Fraser's*, and his *Reliques*, we are told, formed, month by month, the chief attraction of the magazine. The versatility of his genius was astonishing, from the broadest kind of burlesques to the tenderest of lyrics. His favorite amusement, however, among all his surprising literary freaks, was to translate into Latin or French the poems of some well-known English writer, and then to accuse the original author of plagiarism,—see especially *The Rogueries of Tom. Moore.*

Now with such an able contributor, whose audacity knew no bounds, is it surprising to find in *Fraser's* for 1836 these precious ' familiar Letters of Cowley ?' Compare the other articles in the January number, and see how few serious compositions are there. In addition to the Parliamentary Report covering sixty-two pages, mentioned above, there are the following : *Gallery of Literary Characters, No. LXVIII. Regina's Maids of Honor. The Greek Pastoral Poets—Theocritus, Bion, and Moschus* (in which may be clearly seen the pen of Father Prout), *Mr. Alaric Alexander Watts. The Speech of Mr. William Erle, Esqr., K. C., in the case of Watts v. Fraser and Moyes.* Compare also in the December number the letter of Sir Edgerton Brydges to Oliver Yorke (p. 695).

Thus the *prima facie* evidence seems very strong that these Cowley letters were further contributions from the pen of Father Prout, or of one of his associates among that jovial band of *Fraserians.*

Dr. Grosart recognized the value of my material by publishing it in the *Athenaeum* (July 17, 1897) without

2

previously consulting me, and with but scant acknowledg-
ment.

THE DAVID THEME IN LITERATURE PRECEDING COWLEY.
LEGENDS AND TRADITIONS.

In addition to the multiplicity of incidents connected
with David's life in the biblical story, there arose many
legends and traditions concerning him.[1] Among these
may be mentioned : The story of the three historical
stones which cried unto him, as he was on his way to the
camp of the Israelites, to take them with him. He
granted their request, and it was with these three stones
that he smote first Goliath, then the right wing of the
Philistine army, and finally the left wing. How David
invented chain armor, and by means of his coat of mail
was saved from Saul, who attempted to stab him as he
lay sleeping. Of David's wonderfully rapid growth, so
that Saul's armor fitted him perfectly, though he was a
mere stripling. How Satan in the form of a bird leads
David to sin with Bathsheba. Of David and the rhinoce-
ros. Of David and the stag, and how the giant laid a
winepress upon David without injuring him. Of the reed
and bell sent from God to enable David to give confident
judgment in all cases pleaded before him. Finally the
wonderful account of David's death,—how the angel of
Death led the venerable king to climb a tree, and then
meanly took advantage of him by removing the ladder,
so that the good old king, then well stricken in years,
attempting to descend, fell and broke his neck, and so he
died.

With these legends, interesting as they are, the present
investigation has no direct concern, save in so far as they
serve to show the great popularity of the story of David.
All the plays and poems to which I have had access are
based almost exclusively upon the scriptural narrative.

The history of David as contained in the first and

[1] See Migne, *Dictionnaire des Apocryphes*, II, 191 ff. ; Baring-Gould, *Legends
of the Old Testament Characters*, London, 1871.

second books of Samuel has proved a never-failing source of inspiration for early morality plays and for later dramas and poems in the literature of Europe and of England. An enumeration and classification of these plays and poems, such as Alexander von Weilen has made for the Joseph theme,[1] would be a difficult task, beyond the scope of this investigation. What is here attempted, is an enumeration of some of the more important David themes in the poetry and drama of England and of Europe, and a brief review of such as may have directly or indirectly influenced Cowley. The attempt will also be made to show how in the *Davideis*, the David and the Joseph themes came into contact.

That the Biblical history of David was an abundant source of inspiration for later writers is shown in the fact that it branches out into no less than six distinct and important streams: David and Saul (David Persecuted), David and Goliath, David and Jonathan, David and Bathsheba, David and Absalom, and David and Nabal, besides such scenes as the crowning of David, and the marriage of David.

As to the relative popularity of these various episodes, it is difficult to reach a definite conclusion, on account of the limited material to which I have had access. Judged solely by the number of the plays, the persecution of David by Saul and the contest between David and Goliath seem to have been the most attractive themes. Next in importance comes David's adultery with Bathsheba. Alexander von Weilen, *Der ägyptische Joseph*, *vorwort*, points out the fact that three Biblical subjects held almost complete and undisputed possession of the stage during the sixteenth century: namely, The Prodigal Son, Susannah, and Joseph. In the first case, he goes on to show, the dramatic effect is greatest, for here we have real sin to be atoned for, while in the case of Susannah and Joseph we have innocence unjustly accused.

---

[1] See Alexander von Weilen, *Der ägyptische Joseph im Drama des XVIten Jahrhunderts, ein Beitrag zur vergleichenden Litteraturgeschichte*, Wien, 1887.

In close connection with the Prodigal Son among the courtesans and his subsequent repentance, appears David's sin with Bathsheba and his later hearty contrition; and Saul's cruel and unreasonable persecution of David arouses for the latter the same pity among the spectators that would be felt for Joseph and Susannah unjustly accused. Finally, David's victory over Goliath,—the triumph of skill over brute strength, of right over might,—would be of never-failing interest to all classes of people.

The following list, though it does not claim to be complete, is of value in showing the extent and popularity of the David theme in literature preceding Cowley.

FIFTEENTH CENTURY. The earliest extant drama concerning David appears in Rothschild's *Mistère du Viel Testament*, Paris, 1877 ff., IV, 76 ff. It belongs to the end of the 15th century.

SIXTEENTH CENTURY.

1500 *La rapresentatione della distructione di Saul et del piato di Dauit. Finita la rappresentatione della || battaglia de filistei et della distru || ctione di Saul.* s. l. n. d. [vers 1500]. In-4. Again in 1547, 1559, and ca. 1600.

1538 God's Promises, A Tragedye or Enterlude, manyfesting the chefe promyses of God unto Man in all Ages of the olde lawe, from the fall of Adam to the Incarnacyon of the Lorde Jesus Christ. Compyled by John Bale, Anno Domini 1538, 8vo. See Dodsley's *Old Eng. Plays*, London, 1825, I, 1 ff.

David and Absalom, a Tragedy in five acts. Attributed to Bale. See Rothschild, IV, lxxxi ; Halliwell, *Dict. of Old Eng. Plays*, London, 1860, p. 70. (This play, however, is not mentioned among Bale's works.)

1545 Ein schöne tröstliche Historia von dem Jüngling David unnd dem mutwilligen Goliath, gehalten zu wienn inn Osterreich durch wolffgang schmeltzel burger daselbst und Schiilmaister zun Schotten, &c. *Gedruckt zu Wien in Osterreich durch Hans Singriener.* See Rothschild, IV, lxxxiv.

1549 Nabal. Rod. Gualteri Tigurini Comoedia. *Absque nota* [Tiguri circa 1549]. In-8. See Rothschild, IV, lvii. Another edition, Mylium, 1562.

1550 Nabal. Ein schön Christenlich, lustig, vnn Kurtzwylig Spil, erstlich durch den Eerwirdigen vnnd wollgeleerten Herren Rudolffen Walthern, ausz dem ersten buch Samuelis, des 25 Cap. gezogen, in ein Latinische Comediam gestelt, nüwlich aber von einer Eerlichen loblichen Burgerschafft zu Schaffhusen, auff den 16. tag Höwmonats, des 1559 jars, Teütsch gespilt vnnd gehalten. *Getruckt zu Mülhusen im oberen Elsasz durch Peter Schmid. Anno* M.D.LX. In-8. See Rothschild, IV, lviii.

1551   Dasz alle hohe gewaltige Monarchien von Gott eingesetzt vnd geordnet, die grossen mechtigen Potentaten vnd Herrn zu struffen, recht wider gewalt auffzurichten, auch wid' dieselbigen sich niemand setzen, verachten noch emporen soll, wirdt durch das exempel des Künigs Samuelis vnd Saulis klärlich angezeygt . . . durch Wolfgang Schmeltzel Burger zu Wienn. Im 1551 Jar. [at end:] *Gedruckt zu Wienn in Osterreich durch Egidium Adler,* 1551. In-8. See Rothschild, IV, xlv.

1551   Monomachia Dauidis et Goliae.   Tragico-comœdia noua simul et sacra.   Authore Iacobo Schœppero Tremoniano. *Antuerpiœ Ioannes Latius,* 1551.

"*C'est probablement la pièce de Schœpperus qui fut représentée en 1577, par les élèves du gymnase de Copenhague.*" See Rothschild, IV, lix.

1551   Ein tragedi, mit vierzehen personen zu agieren, der auffrhürische Absolom mit seinem vatter, König David ; hat fünff actus.   By Hans Sachs.

[at end:]   *Anno Salutis 1551 jar, am 26 tag Octobris.*   See *Bibl. des Litt. Vereins im Stuttgart,* 110, 86–111.

Comedia mit 10 personen, der David mit Batseba im ehbruch, unnd hat fünff actus.   By Hans Sachs.   Ibid., 131, 319–341.

1552   Tragedia mit 13 personen zu recidirn, wie König David sein mannschaft zelen liess, unnd hat drey actus. By Hans Sachs.   Ibid., 13, 365–401.

[at end :]   *Anno Salutis 1551, am 12 tag Novemb.*

1551 (?)   Tragedie de la desconfiture du geant Goliath. *A Lausanne.* s. d. [1551?]. In-8.   71 pp.   By Joachim de Coignac.   See Migne, *Dict. des Apocr.,* II, 195, note ; Rothschild, IV, lxiv.

1553   Ein comedi, mit acht personen zu recidiren : Die Abigayl, und hat V actus.   By Hans Sachs.

[at end :]   *Anno Salutis* MDLIII *am 4 tag Januarii.* See *Bibl. des Litt. Vereins im Stuttgart,* 173, 70–86.

1554 Ölung Dauidis desz Iünglings, vnnd sein streit wider den Risen Goliath. Durch Valentinum Boltz von Ruffach. *Gedruckt zu Basel, by Bartholome Stähälin*, 1554. See Rothschild, IV, lxxxv.

1555 Goliath, Die Histori wie Dauid der Iüngling den Risen Goliath umbbracht unnd erlegt hat. Ist zu Bern durch ein gemeyne Burgerschaft gespilt. *Gedruckt zu Bern by Samuel Apiario*, 1555. [at end :] Hans von Rüte. In-8. See Rothschild, IV, lxxxv.

1557 Tragedia Mit 14 Personen : die vervolgung König Dauid von dem König Saul. Hat 5 actus. By Hans Sachs. Nürmberg, *1561 ;* dated, however, *6 September, 1557.* See Rothschild, IV, xlv ; *Bibl. des Litt. Vereins im Stuttgart*, 131, 262–318.

1561 A new interlude of the ij synnes of Kynge Davyde, licensed by T. Hackett, 1561–62. See Rothschild, IV, lxxxii ; Warton-Hazlitt, *Hist. Eng. Poetry*, II, 234 ; Hazlitt, *Handbook Early Eng. Lit.*, 1867, under *Plays.*

1562 Finis Saulis et Coronatio Davidis, tragi-comœdia. *" Cette pièce fut représentée avec grand succés par les élèves du Clementinum de Prague le 19 septembre 1562."* See Rothschild, IV, xxv.

1556 Tragedies sainctes. Dauid combattant. Dauid triomphant. Dauid fugitif. Par Loys des Masures Tournisien. *A Geneve, De l'imprimerie de François Perrin.* 1566. In-8. 272 pp. Other editions printed at Antwerp, Geneva, and Paris, in 1582, 1583, 1587, 1595. See Rothschild, IV, lxv.

1567 Tragico-comoedia. Von dem frommen Könige David vnd seinem auffrürischen Sohn Absolon . . . Agiret zu Schwerin auff dem Schlosz für den . . . Herrn Johan Albrecht, Hertzogen zu Meckelnburgk, etc., seiner F. G. Gemahl, Iungen Herren, vnd Frawlin Vrsula, gebornes Frawlin zu Meckelnburg, Eptissin zu Ribnitz, etc. Anno 1567, 1. Sept. [at end :] *Gedruckt zu Lübeck, durch Asswerum Kröger.* MDLXIX. In-8 de 88 pp. *" La dédicace datée de Schwerin, le dimanche de la Trinité 1569, est signée de Bernhard Hederich, prorecteur de l'école de cette ville."* Rothschild, IV, lxxxvi.

1570 Spel van den Koninglyken profect David. Composed

by the painter Charles van Mander. Acted at Meulebeek (Belgium), *ca.* 1570. Rothschild, IV, lxxxii.

1571 Saul. Ein schön, new Spil, von Künig Saul, vnnd dem Hirten Dauid : Wie desz Sauls hochmut vnd stoltz gerochen, Dauids Demütigkeit aber so hoch erhaben worden. Durch ein Eersamme Burgerschafft der loblichen Statt Basel gespilet auff den 5 tag Augustmonats, Anno 1571.

At the end of the dedication appears the name of the author, Mathias Holtzwart de Ribeauvillé (Rappoltzweiler). See Rothschild, IV, xlvi.

1572 Saul le Furieux, // Tragedie prise de la // Bible, // Faicte selon l'art & à la mode des // vieux Autheurs Tragiques. // Plus une Remonstrāce faicte pour le Roy Charles IX, // à tous ses subiects, à fin de les encliner à la paix. // Auec // Hymnes, Cartels, Epitaphes, Anagrammatismes, // & autres œuvres d'un mesme Autheur. // *A Paris* // *Par Frederic Morel Imprimeur du Roy.* // M.D.Lxxii [1572]. Avec Privilege dudit Seigneur. · Prefixed is a discourse *De l'art de la Tragedie* preceded by the name of the author, Jan de La Taille de Bondaroy. The play is written in verse, and is divided into five acts. Several editions appeared ; 1601, 1610. See Rothschild, IV, xxx.

1572 Die schöne biblische historia von dem heil. Königl. Propheten Dauid vnd seinem Sohne Salamo spielweise gestellet, durch Christian Berthold von Brandenburg Stadtschreiber zu Lübben. *Wittenberg,* 1572. In-8. See Rothschild, IV, lxxxvi.

1572 König Davids vnnd Michols Heurath und Hochzeit in ein Comediam gefast durch Johann Teckler. 1572. In-4. See Rothschild, IV, lxxxvi.

1575 'Audict an 1575, les troys jours de la Penthecoste, fut jouée *l'Histoire de David et Golias, jeant,* audevant l'eglise Sainct George, ou y eust grande compaignie de l'eglise, noblesse et habitans de la ville, en grand rejouyssance.'

Quoted from *Mémoires de Jean Burel, bourgeois du Puy, publiés par Augustin Chassaing,* Le Puy-en-Velay, Marchesson, 1875. In-4. Rothschild, IV, lxviii.

1578 Du Bartas. La Sepmaine, ou Creation du Monde. Paris, 1578. See Seconde Semaine, Quatrième Jour.

1579 The Holie Historie of King David ; wherein is chiefly learned those godly and wholesome lessons, that is, to have sure patience in persecution, due obedience to our Prince without Rebellion, and also the true and most faithful dealings of friends. Drawn into English Metre for the youth to reade by John Marbeck. London, 1579. 4to. See Watts, *Bibliotheca Britannica.*

1580 Among works printed by Henry Denham appears David's Sling against great Goliath; a Sword against the Feare of Death; a Battel between the Devill and the Conscience; the Dead Man's Schoole; a Lodge for Lazarus; a Retraite for Sin. London, 1580. 16mo. See Watts, *Bibl. Brit.*

1582 In Historiam Monomachiæ Davidis et Goliathi Inquisitio. By David Hostius, *Ant.*, 1582. 8vo. See Watts, *Bibl. Brit.*

1583 Saul. Trauerspiel, acted in Annaberg, Germany, Feb. 17, 1583. See Rothschild, IV, xlvi.

1584 Du Bartas, La Seconde Sepmaine.

1586 Dauid sconsolato. Tragedia spirituale. Del R. Pier Giovanni Brunetto, frate di S. Francesco osseruante. *In Fiorenza, per Giorgio Marescotti.* 1586. Another edition, Venice, 1605. See Rothchild, IV, lxxii.

1597 David, virtutis . . . probatum Deo spectaculum . . . by Arias Montanus (Benedictus).

Aeneis laminis ornatum a I. T. & I. I. de Bry, etc., with a preface by C. Ritterhusius [Frankfort] 1597. See Cowley's reference to Arias Montanus, *Davideis*, Book II, note 47.

1599 The Love of David and Fair Bethsabe. By George Peele. London, 1599.

1600 Monomachia Davidis cum Goliath, tragoedia sacra.

Tragico-comœdiæ sacræ quinque, ac tres Fabellæ, cum aliquot Epigrammatibus. Authore Gabriele Iansenio, Scholarcha Abstano. Gandani, Ex officina Gualterij Manilij, Typogr. Iurati, ad signum albæ Columbæ. 1600. See Rothschild, IV, lix.

1600 Kurzer Auszzug vnd Summarischer Innhalt, der Tragedi vom König Saul, Vnd Comedien vom König Dauid, ausz H. Schrifft gezogen. . . . Gehalten . . . Inn Dem Fürstlichen Collegio vnd Academia der Societet Iesu in der Steyrischen Haubstatt Grätz den [ ] tag Aprilis, Anno 1600. *Gedruckt zu Grätz, bey Georg Widmanstetter.* S. d. [1600]. In-4to.

Represented on the occasion of the marriage of the Arch-

duke Frederick with the Princess Palatine Marie-Anne. See
Rothschild, IV, xxvi.

1600 Tragédies et autres Œuvres. Par Antoine Mont-
chrestien. Contains five tragedies, among which: *David ou
l'Adultère*, Rouen, 1604, 1606.

1602 Dauid victus et victor.

*Adulterium: Zwo Christliche Spiele vom laster des Ehebruchs.
Von Ambrosio Pape, Pfarrer zu Klein-Ammansleben im Magde-
burgischen* (Magdeburg, 1602). See Rothschild, IV, lxxxvi.

1604 Konungh Da // widhz Historia ifrån thet // han bleff
smordh til Konungh j // Betlehem aff Propheten Samuel, // in
til thes han Kom igen til Ierusalem, // sedhan Absalon dödher
waar, Nyli- // ghen vthsatt pâ rijm. Lustigh // att lasa, etc.
Tryckt j Stockholm, aff Anund // Olufson, Anno 1604. Prose and
verse, in three acts. Author, Thomas Gevaliensis. See Rothschild, IV, xci.

1606 Comoedia von Dauid vnd Goliath. Gestellet durch
M. Georgium Mauritium den Eltern. Von dem Autore mit
Fleisz von newem durchsehen. Leipzig, 1606. See Rothschild,
IV, lxxxvii.

1609 Davide perseguitato. Tragedia di Felice Passero.
In Napole, per Gio : Domenico Roncagliolo, 1609. See Rothschild,
IV, lxxii.

1612 Three sermons wherein Queen Elizabeth is paralleled
with David, Joshua, and Hezekia. London, 1612. 8vo.
By Valentine Leigh. See Watts, *Bibl. Brit.*

1614 Davide, re adultero et micidiale, ma penitente. Rappresentazione di Fra Michiele Zanardo. *In Venezia, per Antonio
Turrini*, 1614. See Rothschild, IV, lxxii.

1616 Ioseph Goetzii eyn geystliche Comedia vom Goliath.
Magdeburg, 1616. See Rothschild, IV, lxxxvii.

1620 Dauidis Ærumnosum Exilium et gloriosum Effugium.
Die Beschwerliche Flucht vnd herliche Auszflucht, des
vnschuldigen Königlichen Hoffdieners Dauids, wie er vom
Könige Saul verfolgt, glücklichen entgangen, vnd an dessen
stadt zum Königreich mit Ehren erhaben worden. In die
Form einer Christlichen Comedien vnd Spiel verfast, Gott zu
Ehren, zum erstenmal agiret zu Baldstedt, auff begehren
etlicher ehrlicher Leute zum Drucke vbergeben. 1620. Von
Tobia Kilio Baldstadensi, Pfarrer zu Eschenberga. *Gedruckt
zu Erffurdt, Bey Tobiæ Fritzschen.* See Rothschild, IV, lxxxvii.

1620 Francis Quarles. Feast of Wormes, etc. 1632 Divine Fancies, edited by A. B. Grosart, *Chertsey Worthies*, 1880–1881.

1628 *a* Dauide. Tragedia dell' Accademico Nascosto [cioè del F. Tancredi Cottone, Sanese, Compagnia di Gesù]. *In Roma, per Guglielmo Facciotti*, 1628. See Rothschild, IV, lxxiii.

b David per Saulis persecutionem ad regnum Israelis erectus. Ex Tancredo Cottono Soc. Jesu.

'*Tragédie en cinq actes qui offre un curieux mélange du sacré et du profane. Les personnages sont : Pluto, Sulphurimis, genius infernalis, Saul, Jonathas, Eliab, Abner, Joab, Mosue, miles, Capitaneus, Moab, Dochim, pastor, Charon, cum Cerbero, Nuncii, Chori.'* Published 1680. See Rothschild, IV, lxxiii.

1630 The Muses Elizium : three Divine Poems on Noah's Flood, Moses' Birth and Miracles, and David and Goliath. By Michael Drayton. London, 1630. 4to.

1631 David's Heinous Sin, Repentances, and heavy Punishments. By Thomas Fuller, D.D., London, 1631. 8vo. See Grosart's edition : *Poems and Translations in verse*, Liverpool, 1868. *Privately printed.*

1632 *a* Il Gigante. Rapprezentazione fatta nel Seminario Romano. Poesia del P. Leone Santi, Sanese, della Compagnia di Gesù. *In Roma, per Francesco Corbelleti*, 1632. See Rothschild, IV, lxxiii.

b Dauide, rappresentazione fatta nel Seminario Romano, e altre poesie del P. Leone Santi, Sanese, della Compagnia di Gesù. *In Roma, per Francesco Corbelletti*, 1637. In-12. See Rothschild, IV, lxxiii.

1633 True Happiness, or King David's Choice. By Wm. Struther. London, 1633.

'Begunne in Sermons, and now digested into a Treatise.'

1634 Davide persequitato. Venetia, 1634. By Marquis Virgilio Malvezzi.

1635 The Story of David and Berseba [a ballad]. 2 pts. Black Letter. London, [1635 ?]. See *Roxburghe Ballads*, I, 88.

1635 David's Diamond Sparkling in the Darke, or A Meditation on part of the ninth Verse of the 36 Psalme. By P. H. London, 1635.

1637 A Translation from Italian into English of Il Davide Persequitato, i. e. David Persecuted. London, 1637. See Watts, *Bibl. Brit.*

1637 Israel // affligé // ou // Tragccomedie // aduenuc du temps // du Dauid, // etc. *A Genève // Par Iacques Planchant,* 1637. With an epistle signed Jean Vallin, Genevois. See Rothschild, IV, lxviii.

Among the dramatis personæ appears *Alecton, furie.*

1637 David, hoc est vertutis exercitatissimæ probatum Deo Spectaculum ex Davidis pastoris, militis regis, exulis, ac prophetæ exemplis. *Consisting of 49 engravings.* Amstelodami, 1637.

1638 Davi[ds] troubl[es] remembered in 1 Absolons Sheepshearing. 2 Joab projecting. 3 Bathsheba bathing. 4 Israel rebelling. 5 Ahitophel hanging. 6 David returning. [a poem]. London, 1638.

The earliest drama of David to which I had access, and possibly the earliest extant, is a French miracle play belonging to the end of the 15th century, and printed in Rothschild's *Le Mistère du Viel Testament*, IV, 76 ff. Over 4000 lines are devoted to the history of David.

The scene opens with a conversation between Jesse and his three sons, Helyas, Amadab, and David, in which he assigns to each his path in life. The two older are to follow the train of ' noblesse,' while the youngest is to become a shepherd. The varying fortunes of David are then set before us, following closely the Scriptural account. But the poet has wisely omitted many tiresome details, and has not hesitated to change the order of events. It is noticeable that the episode of David and Bathsheba is given the most prominence.

BISHOP BALE. *God's Promises.*

Rothschild, IV, lxxxi, includes in his list *David and Absolon*, a tragedy in five acts, by Bishop Bale, mentioned by Halliwell, *Dict. Old Eng. Plays*, London, 1860, p. 70. This was not accessible, but of the other works of Bale, Dodsley, *Old Eng. Plays*, London, 1825, I, ff., prints *God's Promises, A Tragedye or Enterlude, manyfesting the cheefe promyses of God unto man in all ages of the olde lawe, from the fall of Adam to the Incarnacyon of the Lorde Jesus Christ.*

Compyled by Johan Bale, Anno Domini, 1538. 8vo. Doubtless published abroad at Geneva.

The drama is divided into seven acts, corresponding to seven ages or periods, the seven promises of God to Adam, Noah, Abraham, Moses, David, Esaias, and John the Baptist. At the end of each act is a kind of chorus, performed with voices and instruments, and subjoined are a prologue and epilogue, spoken by the author Baleus himself.

Each act is devoted to a dialogue between the Creator and one of the characters. In act 5 appear *Pater Coelestis* and *David, Rex Pius.* God complains to David of the idolatry of Israel and threatens to punish her. David begs him to stay his hand, and refers to all the good men of Israel and their good deeds. The Lord, however, becomes more personal in his accusation, and insists that David himself must be punished for his adultery with Bathsheba. David is then given his choice among three punishments: seven years' famine, three months' exile, or three days' pestilence. David, however, is unable to choose, and leaves all to the Lord, who determines to send a pestilence of three days' length, during which time three score thousand men are to die. David then begs that his innocent people may be spared, and that he, who alone is guilty, may be punished. This pleases the Lord, and he makes a promise to David that the kingdom shall descend to his son, and that this son shall build a temple to the Lord. David then sings a hymn of praise to the Lord, thanking Him for his victories over the bear, the lion, and Goliath.

This miracle play, though very simple in construction, is more ambitious in design than the French mistère, and is developed according to a strict logical plan. The object of the learned Bishop was not so much to amuse as to instruct:

No tryfling sporte
In fantasyes fayned, nor soche like gaudysh gere.
But the thyngs that shall your inward stomake cheare,
To rejoice in God for your justyfycacyon,
And alone in Christ to hope for your salvacyon.

HANS SACHS'S PLAYS.

In Sachs's plays, Saul's Persecution of David, David and Absalom, David and Bathsheba, David and Abigayl, and David numbers his People, are largely paraphrases of the Scriptural text. The poet has added nothing of his own, either by way of material or manner of treatment. On the contrary, the Biblical narrative has suffered at his hands.

DU BARTAS'S WORKS.

Of no little importance in the history and development of the religious epic were the works of Guillaume de Saluste du Bartas, who flourished during the latter half of the XVIth century.[1] Du Bartas was a strong Protestant, and in the great Civil War in France in the time of Charles IX and Henry III, he warmly espoused the cause of the Huguenots. Attaching himself to Henry IV, he aided him on the field and in the council chamber, and was sent as ambassador to the court of Scotland, where King James VI took a great liking to him and wished to retain him in his service. James was an ardent admirer of his poems, and tried his hand at translating *L'Uranie* and *Les Furies*,[2] the third part of the first day; while Du Bartas translated into French a poem of the King's.[3]

Du Bartas, however, remained faithful to King Henry to the last, and at the great battle of Ivry, fought bravely for the royal cause, and received wounds from which he soon afterwards died (1590).

His principal work consists of an almost complete history of the Old Testament in verse. The first part is entitled *La Sepmaine, ou Creation du Monde,* published first at Paris, 1578, 4to. The privilege of the king is dated

[1] See Sainte Beuve, *Revue des Deux Mondes,* 1842, 4th series, vol. 29, pp. 549 ff. ; *Fraser's Magazine,* vol. 26, 1842, pp. 312 ff. ; vol. 58, 1858, pp. 480 ff.

[2] *The Exord, or preface of the second week of Du Bartas. The Furies. His Majesties Poeticall Exercises,* etc., 1591. 4to.

[3] *La Lepanthe de Jacques VI, faicte Francoise par le Sieur du Bartas. His Majesties Poeticall Exercises,* etc., 1591.

Feb., 1578. The second part is entitled *Le Seconde Sep-maine*, and was first published in 1584.

The success of the first part was immediate and striking. It was translated into Latin, Italian, Spanish, Dutch, and English, and went through thirty editions in less than six years, so that the fame and influence of Du Bartas spread abroad over England as well as over Europe. Even Milton was a reader and admirer of the *Divine Weeks*.

Joshua Sylvester, an English poet of some note, translated portions of Du Bartas's poem as early as 1591, only one year after the French poet's death.[1] It was not, however, till 1605 that the first edition of the complete translation appeared. Sylvester was peculiarly fitted for his task. He had acquired a thorough knowledge of French at school, and he had traveled in Holland, France, and Germany. He was a staunch Puritan and must have been in full sympathy with Du Bartas's religious views, so that his work of translation was doubtless a labor of love. At all events, his translation was successful. It won for him the praise of his contemporaries, and served to establish his reputation as a poet.

Sylvester follows the original closely, with an occasional change of name, so as to make the description more suitable to his own country. For instance, Du Bartas likens Eden to Paris, whereas Sylvester compares it to London, ' that it might be more familiar to his meere English and untravell'd Readers.' Moreover, Sylvester occasionally stops to apply the story to some recent political event. The expulsion of Adam and Eve from Paradise, for instance, is applied to the expulsion of the Spaniards from Cadiz. On the whole, however, it is a faithful translation.

Sylvester was not the only English translator of Du Bartas. In 1596 there appeared at London a translation of part of the *Second Week* by the famous Anglo-Saxon

---

[1] See Arber, *Transcript of the Stationers' Register;* Grosart's Sylvester, *Chertsey Worthies*, Memorial-Intro., pp. XII–XIII.

Scholar William L'Isle, with the long and learned Commentary of Simon Goulart Senlisien. A more complete translation by the same scholar, including the end of the fourth book of *Adam* and all of the four books of *Noah*, was published at London in 1625. There were also other translations of portions of this monster poem by J. Winter, London, 1604; Thomas Lodge, 1621; and a Latin rendering at Edinburgh, 1600. Of Du Bartas's *Judith* the translation of T. Hudson appeared at Edinburgh in 1584; London, 1608 and 1611.

The first part of this poem, *La Sepmaine*, is divided into seven days, to represent the week of creation: (1) Chaos. (2) The Elements. (3) The Sea and Earth. (4) The Heavens; Sun, Moon, etc. (5) Tne Fishes and Fowls. (6) The Beasts and Man. (7) The Sabbath. To the edition of 1588 are prefixed the first two chapters of Genesis to serve as the argument of the poem.

This first part, containing more than six thousand lines, is almost encyclopaedic in content. Not satisfied with mentioning hail or snow or wind among the created elements, the poet must enter into a long and involved discussion as to the origin of each; likewise of birds and beasts and fishes; so that Du Bartas has given us a storehouse of mediaeval science and folk-lore. At every opportunity he has stopped to bring in elaborate theological discussions,—for example, as to the essence of God and the nature of the Trinity,—for the aim of the poet has been to instruct as well as to amuse. The poem has been made still more compendious by Simon Goulart de Senlis, who has added to each book a summary at the beginning, marginal notes, and at the end, full explanation of all difficulties.

The second part, *La Seconde Sepmaine*, was also divided into seven days, to form a second week. Here the poet's design was a vast one; he intended to treat the whole Biblical history as contained in the Old and New Testaments. He died, however, before he could carry out his extensive scheme; so that he was enabled to complete only the first four parts, or days of the week.

Each day is devoted to the life of a prophet or of a holy man of Israel: (1) Adam. (2) Noah. (3) Abraham. (4) David. (5) Zedechiah. (6) Messias. (7) Th' Eternall Sabbath. 'But of the three last, Death (preventing Our Noble Poet) hath deprived us.'

The first day is divided into four parts: (1) Eden. (2) The Imposture. (3) The Furies. (4) The Handy-Crafts. Here we have an elaborate treatment of the fall of man. The poet begins with a long description of the Garden of Eden, containing some very pretty passages. Next is narrated how the devil plotteth man's destruction, and clothing himself in a 'Dragon skin, all bright bespeckt,' enters Eden and brings about the fall of man. We are told then of the discord brought about by man's sin, of famine and war and sickness summoned as a result of man's disobedience. Finally the poet relates the first manner of life of Adam and Eve after their fall, and tells of Cain and Abel and of the various useful inventions made by man. The whole occupies nearly three thousand lines in Sylvester's translation.

The second day, Noah, is divided into four parts: (1) The Ark. (2) Babylon. (3) The Colonies. (4) The Columnes.

The third day, Abraham, is divided into four parts: (1) The Vocation. (2) The Fathers. (3) The Law. (4) The Captains.

The fourth day, David, is divided into four parts: (1) The Trophies. (2) The Magnificence. (3) The Schism. (4) Decay.

Du Bartas was a religious poet but not a mystic, and he contended for the use of Biblical themes as the only proper subjects for verse. His *Uranie* is an address to the Heavenly Muse, a powerful plea for the employment of sacred themes in poetry. As a consequence he was extolled as the one 'Qui Musas ereptas profanae lasciviae sacris montibus reddidit; sacris fontibus aspersit; sacris cantibus intonuit.'

In his own words:

> Profanes ecrivans, vostre impudique rime
> Est cause que l'on met nos chantres mieux-disans
> Au rang des basteleurs, des boufons, des plaisans ;
> Est qu'encore moins qu'eux le peuple les estime.
>
> .   .   .   .
>
> Que Christ, comme Homme-Dieu, soit la croupe jumelle
> Sur qui vous sommeillez. Que, pour cheval ailé
> L'Esprit du Trois fois.

Cowley felt the same inspiration of the Heavenly Muse, and declared that the Muse had been debased by poems upon profane and lascivious subjects. 'Amongst all the holy and consecrated things which the Devil ever stole and alienated from the service of the Deity,' are his impassioned words in his general preface to his work, 'there is none so long usurpt as poetry. . . . It is time to baptize it in Jordan, for it will never become clean by bathing it in the waters of Damascus.' His divine mission to purify poetry is also seen clearly in the *Davideis*, I, 37 ff.

> Too long the Muses' land hath heathen been ;
> Their gods too long were devils, and virtues sin,
> But thou, Eternal Word, hath called forth me,
> Th' Apostle to convert that world to thee.

Cowley and Du Bartas had much in common. The French poet gave up his very life to the cause of Protestantism and of his royal master. Cowley was a staunch Royalist, even at the University, and in a few years, he too was to devote his time and his talents to the service of his king. Moreover, as shown above, both had the same conception of the moral purpose of poetry. There was thus much in the life of the French poet to arouse the sympathy of the young Cambridge student. On the whole, then, we should expect to find no slight influence of Du Bartas upon Cowley's religious epic, the *Davideis*.

Of especial interest in connection with the *Davideis* is Du Bartas's history of David as contained in the Fourth Day of the second week, part first, entitled *Les Trophées*. In the preceding part, *Les Capitaines*, the people had demanded a king, Saul had been chosen and anointed (ll. 879 to end). The poet makes much of this election of the King. It is debated in full assembly,—first, a Plebeian makes a declamation for a Democracy, or People-Sway; next, a Reverend Senator speaks for an Aristocracy, or a rule of a chosen synod of the best men; finally, a noble young prince pleads for a Monarchy, or the Sovereignty of a king. Cowley, Book IV, follows the Biblical account more closely. In *Les Trophees*, the history of Saul is continued: In the opening lines, the rejection of Saul is related and the election of David in his stead. The poet states these facts in a few lines, and then proceeds at once to David's visit to the camp of the Israelites and to his contest with Goliath. To this Du Bartas devotes over three hundred lines including many elaborate similes and comparisons. Next the poet recounts Saul's envy of David and Jonathan's love for him. Nothing, however, is said of David's marriage. Much is made of Saul's visit to the witch of Endor, to which about a hundred lines are given, in addition to a disquisition upon the devil and upon evil spirits in general. The poet is careful to show that the shade summoned up by the witch could not have been Samuel, for devils have no power over saints; it must, therefore, have been the Prince of darkness himself that appeared and spoke to Saul. The relation of the death of Saul and of Jonathan occupies only a few lines, and then follows a long enumeration of David's virtues, together with a consideration of the excellence of his Psalms. The rest of the book treats of David's adultery with Bathsheba (ll. 887–1094). The poet, moreover, take occasion to compare to David King James VI of Scotland, to whose court Du Bartas had been sent by Henry IV of France (see above). The book closes with an account of the pestilence inflicted upon David, as a consequence of his sin, and with an application of this pestilence to France; in Sylvester's translation, to England.

The remarks of Simon Goulart de Senlis, the editor of Du Bartas, in his summary prefixed to this book, are of

great importance in connection with the *Davideis*. 'En
ces chapitres,' he writes, 'le S. Esprit nous fait voir les
merveilles de Dieu en l'infirmité de son serviteur David.
Le Poete represente les principaux poincts d'icelle histoire en onze cens vers ou environs, choisissant ce qui lui
a semblé plus digne d'estre compris en l'oeuvre par lui
entrepris. Car une Davideide vaudroit bien le cours
d'une Eneide, ou le nombre des livres de l'Iliade et de
l'Odyssee ensemble si quelque Chrestien et docte poete
François vouloit y employer le temps et l'estude, comme
un si noble et fertile sujet le merite. Mais le Sieur du
Bartas, qui ne vouloit ainsi s'estendre, ains visoit à se
maintenir en sa bienseance accoustumee, s'est convena-
blement enclos en ce cercle d'un petit nombre de vers,
qui comprenent une infinité de choses, sous le nom de
Trophees ou marques des victoires de David; que nous
rapportons à quatre principaux.'

Here we have a suggestion for just such a poem as
Cowley undertook, and undertook on just such a scale as
is here suggested. In fact, the whole design of Cowley's
work, as given by him in his preface, seems very close to
that of Du Bartas. 'I come now to the last part which
is the Davideis, or an heroical poem of the troubles of
David : which I designed into twelve books ; not for the
tribes' sake, but after the pattern of our master Virgil ;
and intended to close all with that most poetical and
excellent elegy of David on the death of Saul and Jonathan, for I had no mind to carry him quite on to his
anointing at Hebron, because it is the custom of heroic
poets (as we see by the example of Homer and Virgil,
whom we should do ill to forsake to imitate others) never
to come to the full end of their story . . . This I say was
the whole design, in which there are many noble and
fertile arguments behind ; as the barbarous cruelty of
Saul to the priests at Nob, the several flights and escapes
of David, with the manner of his living in the Wilderness,
the funeral of Samuel, the love of Abigail, the sacking of
Ziglag, the loss and recovery of David's wives from the

Amalekites, the witch of Endor, the war with the Philistines, and the battle of Gilboa ; all which I meant to inter-
weave, upon several occasions, with the most of the illus-
trious stories of the Old Testament, and to embellish with
the most remarkable antiquities of the Jews, and of other
nations before or at that age.'

Cowley's whole design was thus wonderfully like that
of Du Bartas. Cowley's poem was to be, not simply a
history of David, but a complete history of the Old Testament. At the same time it is to be noted that Cowley's
plan is founded upon the *Aeneid* of Virgil, to whom the
English poet refers in every matter of doubt. Even here,
however, in casting a religious poem in classical, yet
'heathen,' mold, Cowley follows the precedent of Du
Bartas, who had attempted exactly the same thing in his
epic poem *Judith*, entitled by Sylvester, the English translator, *Bethulia's Rescue*. This poem, containing about fifteen hundred lines, was written before the *Divine Weeks*,
possibly about 1565.' It was first translated into English
by F. Hudson, in 1534, before the publication of the
Second Week. The translation was dedicated to King
James, by whom the work was probably suggested. It
was issued in London in 1608, and again in 1611. Hudson's translation contains exactly the same number of
verses as the original text. Sylvester's translation appeared in 1614, under the title *Bethulia's Rescue*.

For the design and execution of his poem, Du Bartas
in his letter to the reader thus excuses himself : 'Ami
lecteur, m'ayant esté commandé par feu tres-illustre &
tres-vertueuse Princesse Ianne, Reine de Navarre, de
rediger l'histoire de Iudith en forme d'un Poem Epique ;
ie n'ai pas tout suivi l'ordre, ou la phrase du texte de la
Bible, come i'ai tasché (sous toutes fois m'eslonger de la
verité de l'histoire) d'imiter Homere en son Iliade, Ver-
gile en son Eneide, & autres qui nous ont laissé des
ouvrages de seblable estoffe, & ce pour rendre de tant

---

[1] See Sainte-Beuve, *Revue des Deux Mondes*, 1842, 4th series, vol. 49. pp.
551 ff.

plus mon oeuvre delectable. Si l'effect n'a respondu à mon desir, ie te supplie de reietter la coulpe sur celle qui m'a proposé un si sterile suict : & non sur moy, qui ne lui pouvois honnestement desobeyer. Tant y a que comme estant le premier de la France, qui par un iuste Poeme ay traicté, en nostre langue, des choses sacrées, i'espere recevoir de ta grace quelque excuse.'

Compare above the quotation made from Cowley's preface : 'which I designed into twelve books ; .... after the pattern of our master Virgil.' But Cowley is much more modest than Du Bartas, and is willing to put the blame of a possible failure where it properly belongs— upon himself. 'I am farre from assuming to myself to have fulfilled the duty of this weighty undertaking,' he continues, 'but sure I am, that there is nothing yet in our Language (nor perhaps in *any*) that is in any degree answerable to the idea that I conceive of it.' Again he expresses himself to similar effect, in note 3 to the *Davideis*, 'for though some in other Languages have attempted the writing a Divine Poem ; yet none, that I know of, has in English.' Thus he completely ignores Peele, Quarles, Drayton, and Fuller, not to speak of others.

Since Cowley and Du Bartas both imitate classical models, their poems have much in common. In both poems, the same devices were used for the relation of past events ; sometimes by narration, as when, in the second book of *Judith*, the Prince of the Ammonites relates to Holofernes the history of Israel, to which more than half of the book is devoted. Similarly in the *Davideis*, the whole of the fourth book is occupied by David's account of the government of Israel. Again, whole histories are wrought in tapestry. In book II, Judith embroiders divine stories, and in book V she sees various histories woven in the arras of the tent. In the *Davideis* likewise this is a favorite device, as in books II and III. In addition to this, Cowley, by means of David's vision, relates a long history of the future. This general resemblance in the outline and in the use of such epic devices is a natural consequence of the employment of the same classical model. The following points, however, seem clearly established by the foregoing investigation : That Du Bartas set the example for Cowley in his treatment of a religious epic in strictly classical form, and that Cowley derived from Du Bartas not only the inspiration for the *Davideis*, but also many helpful suggestions as to style and treatment of the poem.

I have observed the following more specific correspondences between Cowley and Du Bartas :

> And Saul himself, tho' in his troubled breast
> The weight of empire lay, took gentle rest.
>
> *Davideis*, I, 229-230.

Of Pharaoh :

> Who slumbering then on his unquiet couch
> With Israel's greatness was disturbed much.
>
> Sylvester's Translation, Grosart, I, 185.
> 3d Part of 3d Day of I Week, ll. 92-93.

> Swift Jordan started and straight backward fled,
> Hiding among thick reeds his aged head.
>
> *Davideis*, I, l. 237-238.

> Clear Jordan's Selfe in his dry oazie Bed,
> Blushing for shame, was faine to hide his head.
>
> Sylvester's Translation,
> *Bethulia's Rescue*, I, l. 51-52.

Compare also *Davideis*, I, 70 ff., description of Envy and episode of Envy arousing Saul, with Sylvester's Du Bartas, 2d Week, 3d Day, 3d Book, *The Law*, ll. 45 ff., description of Envy, and episode of Envy inciting Pharaoh to rage. Compare, too, with this same passage of Cowley, the pictures of the furies, 2d Week, 1st Day, 3d Book, ll. 234 ff., and the witch of Endor, 3d Week, 4th Day, 1st Book, ll. 624 ff. (see below, p. 49). Finally compare *Davideis*, I, 441 ff., and note on this passage, with Sylvester's Du Bartas, 2d week, 4th Day, 1st Book, *The Trophees*, ll. 417 ff., influence of music ; *Davideis*, IV, 975 ff., Slaughter of Philistines, with *Bethulia's Rescue*, Grosart's Sylvester, VI, 284 ff.

GEORGE PEELE. *Love of David and Fair Bethsabe.* 1599.

In point of chronology, the next play concerning David to which I have had access, is George Peele's *Love of David and Fair Bethsabe, with the Tragedy of Absalon,* printed at London in 1599, by Adam Islip. 4to.[1]

David and Bethsabe is considered Peele's masterpiece. It has much in common with the earlier miracle plays, but it makes a great advance as compared with them. The scene opens with Bethsabe bathing and David above admiring her charms. He sends Cusay to bring her before him, and tells her of his passion. He then commissions Cusay to fetch Uriah from the army. Joab and his hosts next appear, and Uriah returns to the king. Then follows the episode of Ammon and Thamar. Uriah comes before David, who makes him drunk, 'And David joys his too dear Bethsabe.' Bethsabe laments her folly. The next scene is between Nathan and David, wherein David repents of his sin. Absalom slays Ammon. David marches against Rabath and takes the town. He learns of Absalom's crime, but becomes reconciled to him. Absalom, however, rebels, aided by Achitophel. Achitophel's counsel is disregarded, and he slays himself. Joab slays Absalom, and the play closes with David's lament over his son.

Fleay thinks the situations in the play suggestive of Elizabeth and Leicester as David and Bathsheba, Uriah as Leicester's first wife, and Absalom as Mary Queen of Scots. It remained, however, for the masterly hand of Dryden to draw the wonderful parallel between Absalom and Achitophel and the political events of Charles II's reign.

Although Peele follows closely the main features of the Scriptural account, he has made more than a mere paraphrase, or chronicle history of the Bible. He shows considerable imagination, and he allows himself some little

[1] See Fleay, *Eng. Dram.*, II, 153–154; Warton-Hazlitt, *Hist. Eng. Poetry*, II, 234; Hazlitt, *Handbook*, p. 451; Symond, *Shakespeare's Predecessors*, p. 570; Ward, *Eng. Dram. Lit.*, I, 211 ff.

freedom in the treatment of the dialogues. On the whole, he has handled the subject with dignity and propriety.

FRANCIS QUARLES (1592–1644).

Francis Quarles was a man of very different temperament from Peele. He was deeply religious like Du Bartas, and his mind 'was chiefly set upon devotion and study.' Like Du Bartas and Cowley, he too was a Protestant and a strong supporter of the royal cause; but he was altogether of a gloomy and puritanical cast of mind. He is said to have visited King Charles at Oxford in 1644, and doubtless met Cowley there. He died September 8, 1644.

It was chiefly through his *Emblems* that he secured his reputation; but his earliest poems were religious paraphrases of the Bible. His first poem, published in 1620, is entitled *A Feast of Wormes set forth in a Poeme of the History of Jonah*. It is written in heroic couplets, and contains 1784 lines, besides a Proposition of the Whole, an Introduction, and at the end, The General Use of this History. The story follows the Bible closely, chapter and verse being indicated in the margin. The poem is divided into thirteen sections, at the end of each of which appears a pious meditation, in the nature of a commentary or sermon upon the text. His material for these 'meditations' is drawn from the Bible, from the church Fathers, and often from the Latin and Greek poets.

His other religious poems are: *Hadessa, or the History of Queen Esther*, 1621; *Job Militant*, 1624; *The History of Sampson*, 1631; *Solomon's Recantation*, not published till 1645, but doubtless composed at about the same time that his other religious poems were written. In his *Divine Fancies*, 1633, he has several short poems on David: *Saul and David*, II, 9; *David and Goliath*, II, 10; *David's Epitaph on Jonathan*, II, 13; *David's Choice*, II, 27; *David*, II, 48; *Kain and David*, II, 71; *David*, IV, 39.

In his treatment of these different poems, Quarles shows little or no variation; all are equally dull and monotonous, all are written in heroic couplets, and all contain 'pious meditations' interspersed throughout the story.

For the insertion of the 'Meditations,' the poet, in his preface to *Hadessa*, thus justifies himself:[1] 'As for the Manner of this History (consisting of the Periphrase, the adjournment of the Story, and interposition of Meditations) I hope I have not injured the Matter; For in this I was not the least carefull to use the light of the best Expositors authoritatis quorum sum germanus) not daring to go un-led for fear of stumbling. Some say, Divinity in verse is incongruous, and unpleasing: such I referre to the Psalms of David, or the song of his sonne Solomon, to be corrected. But in these lewd times, the salt, and soule of a Verse, is obscene scurrility, without which it seems dull and lifeless. And though the sacred History needs not (as humane do) Poetry to perpetuate the remembrance (being by God's owne mouth blest with Eternity) yet Verse, working so neare upon the soule, and spirit) will oft times draw those to have a History in familiarity, who (perchance) before (scarce knew there was such a book).'

This recalls at once Cowley's eloquent plea for the employment of Scriptural scenes and incidents as proper subjects for poetry. Cowley wishes to 'recover poetry from the service of the devil,' 'to baptize it in Jordan,' and 'to restore it to the kingdom of God.' 'All the books of the Bible are either already most admirable and exalted pieces of poesy, or are the best materials in the world for it. Yet, though they be in themselves so proper to be made use of for this purpose, none but a good artist will know how to do it . . . for if any man design to compose a sacred poem, by only turning a story of the Scripture, like Mr. Quarles's, or some other goodly matter, like Mr. Heywood of Angels, into rhyme, he is so far from elevating of poesy, that he only abases divinity' (Preface of the author).

Very few will dissent from this opinion of Quarles.

[1] Complete works of Francis Quarles, 3 vols., Grosart, *Chertsey Worthies*, 1880, II. 42.

With such narrow views as he had, he could never have produced a work of art. Leaving aside, however, all question as to the merit of Quarles's poetry, it must be admitted that he gave a great impetus to the employment of Scriptural themes as subjects for poetry, and doubtless had no little influence on Cowley in the choice of a religious subject for his epic.

GEORGE SANDYS (1577–1643).

George Sandys wrote several religious paraphrases : *Upon Job ; Upon the Song of Solomon ; Upon the Lamentations of Jeremiah.* These were published in 1638. He is better known, however, by his *Translation of the Psalms*, published in 1636. Cowley, *Preface to Pindarique Odes*, thus refers to this translation : ' The Psalms of David . . . are a great example of what I have said : all the translators of which (even Mr. Sandys himself ; for in spight of popular error, I will be bold not to except him) . . . are so far from doing Honor, or at least Justice to that Divine Poet, that methinks they revile him worse than Shimei.'

GEORGE WITHER (1593–1632) AND GEORGE HERBERT (1588–1667).

In this connection, as doubtless of influence upon Cowley in his choice of a religious theme, mention must be made of George Wither's tremendous undertaking, his proposed *Exercises on the Psalms ;* of his *Songs of the Old Testament, translated into English Measure*, and of his *Psalms of David.* We must also bear in mind the works of ' holy Mr. George Herbert,' for whom doubtless Cowley had a great respect and regard.

MICHAEL DRAYTON. *David and Goliath.*

The earliest work of Michael Drayton (1563–1631) was a metrical rendering of portions of the Scriptures, entitled *The Harmonic of the Church* (or *The Triumphes of the Churche*), published in 1591. It was, for some unknown reason, destroyed, and only one copy, belonging to the

British Museum, is now known to exist. Then appeared his lyrical, pastoral, and historical poems, *Shepherds' Garland, The Barons' War, England's Heroical Epistles, The Owl, Polyolbion, The Battle of Agincourt, Nymphida.* His last poems, like his first, were religious. They were included under the title ' *The Muses Elysium, Lately discovered, By a new way over Parnassus. The passages therein being the subject of Ten sundry Nymphals, Leading three Divine Poems. Noah's Flood, Moses, his Birth and Miracles, David and Goliah.'* 1630.

Although Drayton was a man of unquestioned virtue, he had not the sombre religious character of Quarles. He could look on the bright side of life and was not, like Quarles, continually reflecting upon the unworthiness of man. In fact there is nothing to show that he would turn naturally to Scriptural subjects. That the influence of Du Bartas led him to select such subjects, there can be no doubt. In his *Moses* he dedicates his work to Du Bartas and Sylvester:

> And thou translator of that faithful Muse
> This all's creation that divinely song,
> From courtly French (no travel do'st refuse)
> To make him master of thy genuine tongue,
> Salust to thee and Sylvester thy friend,
> Comes my high poem peaceably and chaste,
> Your hallowed labours humbly to attend,
> That wreckful time shall not have power to waste.

Moreover, he strikes the same note that we heard from Du Bartas, Quarles, and Cowley,—namely, a regret at the debasement of poetry, and a determination to restore it to its proper sphere.

> Muse, I invoke the utmost of thy might,
> That with an armed and auspicious wing,
> Thou be obsequious in his doubt less right
> 'Gainst the vile atheist's vituperious sting.
>
> .   .   .   .
>
> To shew how poesie (simply hath her praise)
> That from full Jove takes her celestial birth,
> And quick as fire, her glorious self can raise
> Above this base abominable earth.

The use of *Jove* here seems a clear indication of the artificiality of his religious feelings. He was writing of such subjects, not because he felt himself moved by the Holy Spirit to reform poetry, but because he thought it best to follow the fashion.

Drayton's *David and Goliah* is written in heroic couplets, and contains about 850 lines. The poem begins with an invocation to the Muse, and then takes up the story at the time when the Almighty, displeased with Saul for sparing King Agag, had resolved to choose a new ruler for Israel. Then follows a long description of David feeding his flock, and in this enumeration of David's personal charms, the poet gives free rein to his imagination.

No mention, however, is made of Saul's daughters, or of the promise Saul made to bestow his daughter's hand on the conqueror of Goliath. The poet has added no episodes, and he tells his story with directness. He has followed his own fancy throughout, and seems to have had no model before him, either classical or modern. Cowley owes nothing directly to Drayton.

THOMAS FULLER. *David's Hainous Sinne.*

The year following the publication of the *Muses Elysium*, appeared *David's Hainous Sinne*, by Thomas Fuller, D.D. The poem is written in stanzas riming a b a b ccc. It is divided into three parts: *David's Hainous Sinne*, 47 stanzas; *David's Heartie repentance*, 26 stanzas; *David's Heavie Punishment*, 71 stanzas.

In the first part, the story is frequently interrupted by moralizations of the poet. Into the second part is introduced a *Proces du Paradis*. The Lord resolves to punish David, and at once all the elements,—fire, air, water, earth,—offer to be the instruments of his vengeance. The Almighty appeases the strife of the elements, and opening the book of life, offers to blot out David's name, but is dissuaded by His Son, the Prince of Peace. At the decision of the Lord to pardon David, the fickle elements rejoice, and now offer to minister to David's pleasure. Nathan is then sent to David and makes the King's 'marble minde to melt.'

This *Proces du Paradis* is clearly a remain of the earlier Miracle Plays.

The third part treats of the episode of Ammon and Tamar, of Absalom's vengeance upon Ammon, of Absalom's revolt and death. 'At the close of this performance,' writes Oldys (Grosart's edition of Fuller, 1868). 'our author, having subsided into the characters of Queen Elizabeth, King James, and King Charles I, and lamented the loss of the Duke of Brunswick, with the discords then in Europe through the wars in the Netherlands, Denmark, etc., he very properly and piously concludes that those grievances may be bewailed by mankind, but till they are reversed by Providence, they are more befitting his *prayers* than his *pen*.'

Although this poem abounds in the quaint and characteristic conceits of Fuller, it is not altogether without merit, and there is no doubt that Cowley read it with appreciation and genuine admiration.

THOMAS HEYWOOD.

That curious work by Thomas Heywood, *The Hierarchie of the Blessed Angels,—Their Names, Orders, and Offices,—The Fall of Lucifer with his Angells*, London, printed by Adam Islip, 1635, is of some interest in connection with the *Davideis*. That Cowley was familiar with this work is shown by a humorous reference to Heywood (General Preface of the Author), as 'Mr. Heywood of Angels, whose poem serves only to abase divinity' (see above, p. 37).

The *Hierarchie of the Blessed Angels* is a poem in nine books, entitled respectively : *The Seraphim, The Cherubim, The Thrones, The Dominations, The Vertues, The Powers, The Principats, The Arch-Angel, The Angel*. To each book is prefixed the argument in verse, and to each of these arguments is added the name of an angel, as follows :

Uriel, Jophiel, Zaphiel, Zadchiel, Haniel, Raphael, Car-mael, Michael and Gabriel. In addition to this, there are long and elaborate notes, 'Theological, Philosophical, Moral, Poetical, Historical, and Emblematical Observa-tions.' This work, containing over six hundred pages in folio, is a mass of learned references and childish supersti-tions. In the sixth book, *The Powers*, the poet after de-scribing the revolt and fall of the angels, gives descrip-tions of hell drawn from the Bible, from the church fathers, and from the Latin and Greek poets. In his notes to this book he enters into a long discussion as to the nature of hell-fire and as to the torments of the damned, interspersing throughout marvelous ghost tales of Incubi and Succubi.

Although the literary value of Heywood's poem is very slight, and although every one will agree in Cowley's opinion that he serves only to 'abase divinity,' he has nevertheless collected much curious information of no slight value to the writer of a religious epic such as Cowley undertook.

ROBERT ASHLEY'S TRANSLATION OF V. MALVEZZI'S *Il Davide Perseguitato*.

In the year 1637 (doubtless the very year in which Cow-ley was writing his epic), appeared at London Robert Ashley's translation of V. Malvezzi's *Il Davide Perseguitato*. Ashley was a school-fellow of Joshua Sylvester's at Sara-via's school in Southampton, and may have been inspired to translate Malvezzi through Sylvester's translation of Du Bartas.

Malvezzi was for a time in the service of Philip IV of Spain, who sent him to England as his Ambassador. On account of ill-health, however, he was forced to return to his native land, Italy, where he died at Bologna, Aug. 11, 1654. His *Davide* was first published at Bologna in 1634, and again at Venice, 1636. It was translated into French by Louys de Benoist, Avignon, 1646, and into Latin in

1660. Of Robert Ashley's English translation, subsequent editions appeared in 1647 and in 1650.

In spite of this array of editions and translations, Malvezzi's work was only a running commentary, or set of homilies, on the various incidents of David's life. The author holds up the disobedience of Saul as a warning to princes, and contrasts it with the humility of David.

FELICE PASSERO.

Il David Perseguitato, Tragedia, published at Naples in 1609. Inaccessible. Not in British Museum.

Mention must be made here of the curious set of engravings illustrating David's life, entitled: *David, Hoc est Virtutis exercitatissimae Probatum Deo Spectaculum, ex Davidis Pastoris, Militis, Regis, Exulis, ac Prophetae, Exemplis*, Amsterdam, 1637. Each plate is accompanied by a short Latin verse of four lines, similar to the English *Emblems*. This is based upon the more elaborate work of Arias Montanus with the same title, dated 1597. In Montanus, the verses are the same, but the plates are different, and in addition there is with each engraving a *Paraphrasis*, or *Explicatio*. In note 47, Book II of the *Davideis*, Cowley has a reference to Arias Montanus, quoting his opinion in regard to the heathen god Moloch.

DAVID'S TROUBLES, ETC. 1638.

Rather a poor series of poems on David was published in 1638 at London, entitled: *David's Troubles Remembered in:* (1) *Absolon's Sheepshearing;* (2) *Joab projecting;* (3) *Bathsheba bathing;* (4) *Israel rebelling;* (5) *Ahithophel hanging;* (6) *David returning.*

The first book begins:

I tell the divers tryalls of the King
Who hevenly hymns did to his Maker sing:
Blest spirit that infus'd on him such skill,
Dispose aright thine humble servant's quill.

REMARKS ON THE GROWTH OF THE ENGLISH RELIGIOUS EPIC PRIOR TO MILTON AND THE PART PLAYED BY COWLEY IN THIS DEVELOPMENT.

The English religious narrative poem growing out of the lives and legends of the saints, later developing into the English religious epic and reaching its most perfect form in Milton's *Paradise Lost*, must have influenced the miracle plays and been in turn influenced by them. It has been seen how the influence of the miracle plays persisted even through the first quarter of the seventeenth century (see Fuller, *David's Hainous Sinne*, above). In the miracle plays there appear early two different lines of treatment, popular and didactic. Treated in a popular way, these plays were intended solely to amuse ; treated in a didactic way, they came into contact with the homily and the long religious poem like the *Cursor Mundi*, itself a precursor of Du Bartas's *Divine Weeks*. The Old French *Mistère* (above, p. 23) is largely didactic. The poet endeavors all through to make clear the connection between the Old and the New Testament. In the Chester Plays, an Expositor appears between acts and explains the allegorical meaning of the action. This, in fact, was the primary object of the early religious drama, to instruct ; to bring certain facts and dogmas of the Bible within reach of the common mind.

In addition to this, the *Moralities* often became bitterly controversial, as for example in N. Wood's *Conflict of Conscience*, 1581, in which the hero, Philologus, becomes ensnared in the foils of Rome (Ward, *Eng. Dram. Lit.*, 1, 47). Bale's play *God's Promises* is learned and didactic, written for the sole purpose of developing a theological argument.

Du Bartas's poems likewise are both didactic and controversial. In the opening lines of the *First Week*, 1st Day, 1st Part, the poet 'refute par diverses raisons la curieuse et profane objection des atheistes, qui demandent que Dieu faisoit avant qu'il creast le monde.' In the first part of the second day of the second week, he enumerates twelve answers of Noah to the blasphemies of Cham and of his fellow atheists. In that same book he replies at length to the objections of the atheists who contended that the capacity of the ark was insufficient for Noah, his family, and all brute creation.

This introduction of theological argument into a professedly narrative poem is a serious hindrance to the highest artistic development, a blot from which even Milton's epic is not free.

At the close of the sixteenth century, the protest against the growing immorality of the stage was extended to poetry, and Du Bartas (as seen above) makes a powerful plea for the rescue of poetry from profane hands, and for the employment of scriptural themes alone as proper subjects for verse. Thus at the opening of the 17th century, the use of Biblical stories and episodes as proper subjects of verse was a live question in all countries. In France there was the great struggle between the Catholics and Huguenots. Italy was under the tyranny of the popes and of Philip the Second of Spain, and had to furnish Philip with money and men to aid him in his career of bigotry and persecution. The whole of Europe was soon engaged in a great religious struggle, the Thirty Years' War, and England in the time of Cowley and Milton was to be torn asunder by civil strife for political and religious freedom. Men's minds were, therefore, prepared for religious poems, and the appropriateness of such themes as Saul's Persecution of David must have been felt. Malvezzi's *Il Davide Perseguitato*, with its warning to Princes, went through several editions in his country, 1634, 1636, ff., and was translated into Latin and English.

In England during the early part of the 17th century, the soil proved fruitful for religious poems. A year after Du Bartas's death, Sylvester began his translation, and collective editions of it appeared in 1605, 1608, 1611, 1613, 1614, 1621, 1633, and 1641. William L'Isle, the Anglo-Saxon scholar, thought it worth while to translate Du Bartas, and his rendering appeared in 1596, to be followed

4

by a more complete one in 1625. Other translations were made by Winter, and several translations of *Judith* were published by Hudson, all before 1612. Robert Ashley's translation of Malvezzi appeared in 1637.

Among all these religious poems, however, the David theme was not the least popular in England. There were poems of David by George Peele, 1599; Francis Quarles, 1620 ff., *Divine Fancies*, (1633); Michael Drayton, 1630; Thomas Fuller, 1631; yet from Bale to Heywood, no attempt had been made at the true epic form. The aim of the poet was either to make a mere paraphrase of the scriptures, hoping thus to popularize the Sacred Word; or to expound the Holy Writ, using the words of the Bible as his text, like Quarles, 'not daring to go unled.' Peele, Drayton, and Fuller, though far in advance of Quarles, and though showing originality of treatment, made no attempt to produce a finished epic. To Cowley, then, inspired by the example of Du Bartas, must be given the credit of having first attempted the true epic form. His conception was a noble one, but his powers were not equal to the task.

COWLEY AND MILTON.

As an outcome of this great interest in religious themes was written the most perfect religious epic of modern times, the *Paradise Lost*. Milton was undoubtedly familiar with Cowley's epic, and Cowley's modest words at the conclusion of his preface seem almost prophetic of that great poem which was so completely to overshadow his. 'I shall be ambitious of no other fruit from this weak and imperfect attempt of mine, but the opening of a way to the courage and industry of some other persons who may be better able to perform it thoroughly and successfully.' In 1658, two years after the publication of these words, Milton settled down to the composition of the *Paradise Lost*, although, it is true, he had already sketched out a plan nearly twenty years before.

Masson (*Life of Milton*, London, 1880, V I, 557), in discussing Milton's relation to his predecessors, remarks:

'Had it been worth while, it could have been proved from *Paradise Lost* that Milton was no stranger to the writings of Cowley and Davenant.'

I have noted the following correspondences between the *Davideis* and the *Paradise Lost :*

Cowley's description of Goliath's spear, *Davideis*, III, 393; and Milton's description of Satan's spear, *Paradise Lost*, I, 292. Both poets, however, borrowed from Homer's description of Polyphemus, *Odyssey*, IX, 367 ff., and Virgil's *Aeneid*, III, 659.

Compare also Cowley's list of false gods, Moloch, Osiris, Dagon, etc., *Davideis*, II, 501 ff., with *Paradise Lost*, I, 393, though it is to be noted that Milton had already used this same catalogue of heathen deities in his *Nativity Ode* (1629), Stanzas XXII–XXIV.

Finally compare Cowley's description of hell, *Davideis*, I, 71 ff., with *Paradise Lost*, I, 56–69. The weakness of Cowley's labored effort, full of his characteristic conceits, is only too evident beside Milton's picture of the vastness and horror of the gloomy abyss.

Though the *Paradise Lost* thus owes directly little or nothing to the *Davideis*, nevertheless Cowley's ideals were lofty, and his very failures may have proved instructive to Milton.

The next section is devoted to a consideration of certain poems concerning David subsequent to Cowley's.

POEMS CONCERNING DAVID SUBSEQUENT TO COWLEY'S.

The *Davideis*, though begun in 1637, was not published till 1656, when it appeared in the first collective edition of his works. The great interest taken in religious poems at this period is still further shown by the fact that another epic poem of the troubles of David, called also the *Davideis*, was begun and written a few years after Cowley's. The author was the well known Thomas Ellwood (1639–1713), the Quaker and the friend of Milton. He entered into numerous religious controversies and published several volumes. Among them were *Sacred His-*

tory, or the *Historical Part of the Holy Scriptures of the Old
Testament*, published in 1705 ; *Sacred History, or the Histor-
ical Part of the Holy Scriptures of the New Testament*, pub-
lished in 1709. His *Davideis* was first published in 1712.
In his Epistle to the Reader, he refers to Cowley's poem :
' Till I had wholly finished and transcribed also this poem,
I had not had the opportunity of perusing the learned
Cowley's *Davideis*, though I had heard of it and I think
had once a transient sight of it, before I began this.
Since, I have read it through with my best attention, and
am very well pleased that I had not read it before : lest his
great name, high style, and lofty fancy should have led
me, unawares, into an apish imitation of them ; which
doubtless would have looked very oddly and ill in me,
how admirable soever in him.

' His aim and mine differ widely : The method of each
no less. He wrote for the learned ; and those of the
Upper Form : and his flights are answerable. I write for
Common Readers, in a style familiar, and easy to be
understood by such. His would have needed (if he had
not added it) a large Paraphrase upon it ; to explain the
many difficult passages in it. Mine, as it has none, will
not, I hope, need any.' And then, in a tone of self-depre-
ciation, he adds what might be construed into a humorous criticism of Cowley and his school : ' I am not so
wholly a stranger to the writings of the most celebrated
poets, as well ancient as modern, as not to know, that
their great embellishments of their poems consist mostly
in their extravagant and almost boundless fancies ; amaz-
ing and even dazzling flights ; luxurious inventions ; wild
hyperboles ; lofty language ; with an introduction of
angels, spirits, demons, and their respective deities, etc.,
which, as not suitable to my purpose, I industriously
abstain from.'

Nevertheless the first book begins in proper classic
style, with the proposition and invocation :

> I sing the Life of David, Israel's King,
> Assist, thou Sacred Power, who didst him bring
> From the sheepfold and set him on the throne.

It contains five books, and is written in heroic couplets. More than twenty years the author had the work on hand, having been interrupted by various disturbances in the kingdom ; but so attractive did he find his subject, that he was led on to finish it, and weave into his poem the complete history of David. In spite, however, of this long process of incubation, the poem possesses very little merit.

Although I have made no effort to trace David poems in the literature of the eighteenth and nineteenth centuries, it may be of interest to call attention to a David epic published in London in 1817. It is entitled : *The Royal Minstrel, or The Witcheries of Endor, an Epic Poem in eleven books, by J. F. Pennie, Dorchester, Printed and sold by G. Clark, 1817.* One of the author's mottoes on the title page is a quotation from Cowley's Preface: ' All the books of the Bible are either most admirable and exalted pieces of Poetry, or are the best materials in the world for it.' The opening scene in the first book seems clearly modelled upon Cowley. The Witch of Endor in a general assembly of Demons and Weird Sisters holds a consultation on the best means of overthrowing Saul. Satan rehearses what he has done against the seed of Israel since he heard in heaven that Christ was to spring from the seed of Abraham. Adramelec informs the infernal assembly that Saul is for his obstinacy rejected by his God, and that another is already chosen to succeed him on his throne ; that this new favorite is David, from whom the Messiah is to spring. They with united power, therefore, resolve to destroy David. Adramelec enters into Saul and incites his rage against David, but David is protected by his guardian angel, Abdiel. The poem ends with the death of Saul and coronation of David. The poem is written in blank verse, and extends through eleven books. It is far superior to Ellwood's labored effort, and contains many fine passages.

In other countries, too, the interest in religious poems continued. At Paris in 1660 was published *David, poeme heroique*, in eight books by le Sieur Lesfargues. It begins in proper classic style :

> Je chante dans l'ardeur du beau feu qui m'anime
> Le Berger Couronné, le vainqueur magnanime
> Du Géant Philistin avec honte abatu :
> Je chante ce David qui seul a combattu.

Five years later, 1665, there appeared at Paris another similar poem ; *David ou la Vertu Couronnée*, par Jacques de Coras, in seven books. It opens similarly :

> Je chante le Berger, le Prince, et le Prophète
> Dont la voix, dont le zèle, et le forte houlète
> Des climats Palestins, par cents climats divers,
> Portèrent la louange au bout de l'Univers.

In the third book there is a picture of the Almighty seated in the Heavens. The Devil appears before him, and begs for permission to enter into Saul's mind. The figures of God and of His Son are extremely puerile.

Finally, in 1691, at Brescia in Italy was published a poem entitled *Davide Ré, poema eroico*, etc., by Count Giovanni Albano.

THE DAVIDEIS IN ITS RELATION TO CRASHAW'S SOSPETTO D'HERODE.

Although critics,[1] in discussing possible sources for the *Paradise Lost*, have brought in many parallels from other poems,—among them from Cowley's *Davideis*, and from Crashaw's *Sospetto D'Herode*,—no one seems to have noted that Cowley and Crashaw, in their descriptions of hell, have both treated the same episode from Virgil, and that their manner of treatment is wonderfully similar. The episode in question is Virgil's account, in the seventh book of the *Aeneid*, of Juno's descent into hell, and of how Alecto, at the command of the goddess, taking her

---

[1] Voltaire, Lauder, Dunster, Hayley, and Masson ; George Edmondson, *Milton and Vondel: a Curiosity of Literature*, London, 1885; August Müller, *Über Milton's Abhängigkeit von Vondel*, dissertation, Berlin, 1891.

snakes incites to rage and madness first Queen Amata and then Turnus.

I purpose, then, in the following pages, to make a detailed comparison of Cowley and Crashaw.

Cowley begins his long epic with the proposition of the whole and the invocation, in proper classic style. The poet then tells of the new agreement that had been entered into between David and Saul. Here, beginning with the seventieth line of the *Davideis* and extending to the three hundred and forty-second, is the passage to be compared with the *Sospetto D'Herode*.

First is shown a picture of hell, which the poet describes at some length. Satan himself is then represented, furious over the friendship which has just been declared between Saul and David. He sees the beauties of young David, and knowing that from him is to spring the Eternal Shiloh, his rage is increased ten-fold. He knocks his iron teeth, he howls, he lashes his breast with his long tail, and he makes hell too hot even for the fiends themselves. He calls upon his hosts for aid to bring to utter ruin 'this bold young shepherd boy.' All the powers of hell at first stand amazed and terrified; the snakes cease to hiss and the tortured souls fear to groan. At last Envy crawls forth from the dire throng, her locks attired with curling serpents, vipers preying upon her breasts, her garments stained with gore, and lashing herself with her knotted whip. Addressing the Arch-fiend at some length, she urges him not to despair, and offers him her aid. Beelzebub, descending from his burning throne, embraces her. She, bowing thrice, sets out at dead of night, and comes to the palace where Saul lies sleeping. All nature shudders at sight of her. Taking upon her the shape of Father Benjamin, she enters the chamber of Saul, and standing by his bedside, urges him to bestir himself and take vengeance upon 'this upstart youth, this beardless shepherd boy.' Then drawing forth one of her worst, her best beloved snakes, she thrusts it into Saul's bosom, and unseen takes her flight into the darkness. Saul awakes in terror, the sweat bedewing his bed. His anger against David is increased ten-fold, and he swears eternal vengeance against him.

Now in Crashaw's *Sospetto D'Herode*, we have exactly the same situation. After invoking the Muse, the poet gives a short description of hell. Next Satan is described. He has heard of God's plan to redeem mankind by sending His Blessed Son to earth. His rage exceeds even that of Cowley's devil. He gnashes his teeth, and lashes his sides with his tail ; he claws his furrowed brow, and finally chews his twisted tail for spite. He summons his hosts to help him. Cruelty appears and offers her services. Her fearful palace is described. Hardly could the Arch-fiend tell her all his intentions, so eager is she for wicked deeds. Rising through the air, she sets out for Bethlehem. Laying aside her own shape, she personates a mortal part, and assumes the shape of Joseph, King Herod's dead brother. Entering the palace, where Herod lies sleeping, she approaches his bed-side. Addressing him in a feigned voice, she urges him to be a man, and to guard himself against the dangers that threaten his kingdom. This said, she takes her richest snake, and, applying it to the king's breast, hastens away. Herod awakes in terror. His bed is bedewed with sweat. In rage he calls for arms and defies his own fancy-framed foes.

Since both accounts are based upon Virgil, the general outline is, of course, the same in each. When, however, we come to compare the details of treatment, we find a striking similarity.

In his description of hell, Crashaw has :

> Below the bottom of the great abyss,
> There where one center reconciles all things,
> The world's profound heart pants ; there placed is
> Mischief's old master ; close about him clings
> A curl'd knot of embracing snakes that kiss
> His correspondent cheekes ; these loathsome strings
>   Hold the perverse prince in eternal ties
>   Fast bound since first he forfeited the skies.

Cowley has similarly :

> Beneath the silent chambers of the earth,
> Where the sun's fruitful beams give metals birth,
> There is a place, deep, wondrous deep below,
> Which genuine night and horror does o'erflow.
>
> .   .   .   .   .   .
>
> Here Lucifer the mighty captive reigns,
> Proud midst his woes, and tyrant in his chains.

Continuing, Crashaw describes the Devil's rage :

> his teeth for torment gnash,
> While his steel sides sound with his tail's strong lash.

Cowley has :

> Thrice did he knock his iron teeth, thrice howl,
> And into frowns his wrathful forehead roll :
>
> .   .   .   .
>
> With that, with his long tail he lashed his breast.

In each poem the Devil has a vision of fate hostile to
him. He sees the promised Shiloh that is to save mankind.

In Crashaw it is expressed thus :

> He calls to mind the old quarrel . . .
>
> .   .   .   .   .   .
>
> Heaven's golden winged herald late *he saw*
> To a poor Galilean virgin sent.
>
> .   .   .   .   .   .
>
> *He saw* the old Hebrew's womb neglect the law
> Of age and barrenness.
>
> .   .   .   .   .   .
>
> *He saw* rich nectar-thaws release the rigour
> Of th' icy North . . .
>
> .   .   .   .   .   .
>
> *He saw* a vernal smile sweetly disfigure
> Winter's sad face.
>
> .   .   .   .   .   .
>
> *He saw* how in that blest day-bearing night
> The Heaven-rebuked shades made haste away.
>
> .   .   .   .   .   .
>
> *He marked* how the poor shepherds ran to pay
> Their simple tribute to the babe.
>
> .   .   .   .   .   .

He saw a three-fold sun, with rich increase,
Make proud the ruby portals of the East ;
He saw the temple sacred to sweet peace
Adore her Prince's birth . . .
He saw the falling idols all confess
A coming deity ; *he saw* the nest
Of pois'nous and unnatural loves, earth-nurst,
Touch'd with the world's true antidote, to burst.

.   .   .   .

He saw heaven blossom with a new-born light, etc., etc.
Struck with these great concurrences of things,
Symptoms so deadly unto death and him,
Fain would he have forgot what fatal strings
Eternally bind each rebellious limb.
He shook himself and spread his spacious wings,
Which, like two bosomed sails, embrace the dim
   Air with a dismal shade ; but all in vain,
   Of sturdy adamant is his chain.

Now in Cowley, the Devil sees in the same way young
David and the promised Messiah to spring from his stock.
The form of the description and the repetition of the
phrase *he saw*, ll. 109 ff. are noteworthy:

He saw the beauties of his shape and face,

.   .   .   .

He saw the nobler wonders of his mind,

.   .   .   .

He saw . . .
How by his young hand their Gathite champion fell.
He saw the reverend prophet boldly shed
The royal drops round his enlarged head.
And well he knew what legacy did place
The sacred sceptre in bless'd Judah's race,
From which th' Eternal Shiloh was to spring,
A knowledge which new hells to Hell did bring ;
And though no less he knew himself too weak
The smallest link of strong wrought fate to break,
Yet would he rage and struggle with the chain.

In the *Sospetto*, Satan addresses his hosts in these words :

And yet, whose force fear I ? Have I so lost
Myself? my strength too, with my innocence ?
Come, try who dares, Heav'n, earth, what'er dost boast
A borrowed being, make thy bold defence.
Come, thy Creator, too ; what though it cost
Me yet a second fall, we'd try our strengths.
   Heaven saw us struggle once, as brave a fight
   Earth now shall see and tremble at the sight.

Cowley's Satan exclaims:

> Are we such nothings then, said he, our will
> Cross'd by a shepherd's boy? And you yet still
> Play with your idle serpents here? Dares none
> Attempt what becomes furies? Are ye grown
> Benum'd with fear or virtue's sprightless cold,
> Ye who were once (I'm sure) so brave and bold?

At the sight of the fury passing through the air, Nature herself is terrified, and Crashaw thus describes it:

> Heaven saw her rise and saw hell in the sight,
> The fields' fair eyes saw her and saw no more,
> But shut their flow'ry lids; forever night
> And winter strow her way: yea such a sore
> Is she to Nature, that a general fright,
> An universal palsy spreading o'er
>   The face of things, from her dire eyes had run
>   Had not her thick snakes hid them from the sun.

Cowley's description is close to this:

> The silver moon with terror paler grew
> And neighb'ring Hermon sweated flow'ry dew.
> Swift Jordan started and straight backward fled,
> Hiding among thick reeds his aged head.

Also see above under Du Bartas. Compare *Aeneid*, VII, 514 ff., referred to by Cowley in note; *Thebaid*, I, 197 ff. (see below).

In the *Sospetto*, Cruelty, personating Joseph, urges Herod to action and exclaims:

> Why did I spend my life and spill my blood,
> That thy firm hand forever might sustain
> A well-pois'd sceptre? Does it now seem good
> Thy brother's blood be spilt, life spent in vain?

In the *Davideis*, Envy, personating Benjamin, thus incites Saul:

> Why was I else from Canaan's famine led?
> Happy, thrice happy, had I there been dead,
> Ere my full loins discharged this numerous race.

Crashaw continues:

> So said, her richest snake, which to her wrist
> For a beseeming bracelet she had tied,
> A special worm it was, as ever kiss'd
> The foamy lips of Cerberus, she applied
> To the King's breast—
> This done, home to her hell she hied amain.

Compare Ovid, *Meta*, VII, 402 ff.; Cowley, *Book of Plants*, III, 195–196.
While Cowley has:

> with that she takes
> One of her worst, her best beloved snakes:
> 'Softly, dear worm, soft and unseen,' said she,
> 'Into his bosom steal and in it be
> 'My viceroy.' At that word she took her flight,
> And her loose shape dissolved into the night.

The effect of this fearful apparition is in each case the same.
In Crashaw:

> He wakes, and with him ne'er to sleep, new fears;
> His sweat-bedewed bed had now betray'd him
> To a vast field of thorns; ten thousand spears
> All pointed at his heart seem'd to invade him;
> So mighty were th' amazing characters
> With which his feeling dream had thus dismay'd him.
>   He his own fancy-framed foes defies;
>   In rage, My arms! Give me my arms! he cries.

In Cowley:

> Th' infested King leaped from his bed amaz'd,
> Scarce knew himself at first, but round him gaz'd.
> And started back at pieced-up shapes which fear
> And his distorted fancy painted there.
> Terror froze up his hair and on his face
> Showers of cold sweat roll'd trembling down apace;
> Then knocking with his angry hands his breast,
> Earth with his feet, he cries: 'Oh! 'tis confess'd,
> 'I've been a pious fool, a woman-King!'

As Crashaw's *Sospetto* is a translation of the first book of Marini's *Strage degli Innocenti*, the first question that arises is, did Cowley borrow from Marini? This can easily be settled by comparing a few passages.

Crashaw describes Satan thus :

His eyes, the sullen dens of death and night
Startle the dull air with a dismal red.

Cowley's description is :

His eyes dart forth red flames which *scare* the night.

In both poets, we see the idea of terror inspired by Satan's eyes. But Marini has :

Negli occhi, ove mestizia alberga e morte
Luce fiammeggia torbida e vermiglia. St. 7.

Again, in describing the effect of the Fury's appearance, Crashaw has :

Such to the *frighted* palace now she comes.

In Cowley we read :

Lo ! at her entrance Saul's strong palace *shook.*

Marini, on the other hand, says merely :

Ricerca e spia della magion reale.

Nothing whatever is said of the effect of her appearance upon the palace.

To take another example, Cruelty, in Crashaw, addresses Herod :

Why dost thou let thy brave soul lie suppressed
In *death-like* slumbers, while thy dangers crave
A waking eye and hand ?

Cowley similarly :

Arise, lost King of Israel ; canst thou lie
Dead in this sleep, and yet thy last so nigh ?

Marini, however, differs from both :

Te ne stai neghittoso, e'l cor guerriero
Nell' ozio immergi e nel riposo i sensi.

The expression 'death-like' belongs only to the English translation.

Finally, in Crashaw, Cruelty says to Herod:

> O, call thyself home to thyself . . .
> . . . . . rouse thee and shake
> Thyself into a shape that may become thee:
> *Be Herod.*

In Cowley, Envy exclaims to Saul:

> Betray not, too, thyself; take courage, call
> Thy enchanted virtues forth and *be whole Saul.*

In Marini simply:

> Sveglia il tuo spirto addormentato, ond'arda
> Di regio sdegno e l'ire e l'armi appresta.

Clearly, then, Cowley did not refer to Marini. That both Marini and Cowley drew from Virgil in the first instance there is not the least doubt, but a common origin does not account for such verbal correspondences as have been shown between Cowley and Crashaw. The question now remains, did Cowley imitate Crashaw? or was Crashaw indebted to Cowley? The difficulty in deciding this question lies in the fact that it is impossible to fix an exact date for Crashaw's translation. The first book, at least, of the *Davideis* was written while Cowley was at Cambridge, 1637–1643. Now Crashaw's *Steps to the Temple*, in which the *Sospetto* appeared, was not published till 1646, just before he left England; yet there is no doubt that he wrote the great body of his poems while he was still at Cambridge. His first publication consisted of some Latin verses on the King's recovery from small-pox (1632), on the King's return from Scotland (1633), and on the birth of James, Duke of York (1633). In 1634 appeared anonymously *Epigrammatum Sacrorum Liber*.

In 1636 Crashaw removed from Pembroke Hall to Peterhouse and was elected a fellow there in 1637, the very year that Cowley entered the University (see above, p. 2).

The first dated editions of Marini's work, *Strage degli Innocenti*, appeared at Rome and at Venice in 1633, although other undated editions had been published before. There was thus ample time for Marini to become known in England, and for Crashaw to make his translation before leaving Cambridge.

As Cowley wrote most of the *Davideis* at Cambridge between 1637-1643 and did not publish it till 1656, so I would assume that Crashaw made his translation at Cambridge just before Cowley's admission to the University, or even while Cowley was a student there, and that it remained in manuscript till 1646, when it was published in the *Steps to the Temple*.

The proofs are not conclusive, it must be confessed, but it seems more probable that Cowley, the younger poet just entering the University, should have borrowed from a translation of the popular Marini (provided it was then in MS.) rather than that Crashaw with his original before him should have borrowed from Cowley's poem.

This episode in the seventh book of the *Aeneid*, in which Alecto, sent by Juno, goes in disguise and arouses the fury of Queen Amata and of Turnus against Aeneas and the Trojans, and upon which Cowley and Marini based their accounts, has been exceedingly popular, and has been imitated again and again both by the Latin and English poets.

COWLEY AND VIRGIL.

Virgil's account, upon which all the episodes to be considered are based, must first be examined in detail. It appears in the *Aeneid*, Book VII, ll. 286 ff. Compared with Crashaw and Cowley, Virgil's description offers a parallel complete in every detail.[1]

Juno sees the success of Aeneas and the Trojans settled in the country of Latium, and knows that the descendants of Aeneas are to possess the land, just as the Devil, in

---

[1] The following paraphrase is based upon *Works of Virgil in Prose* translated by James Davidson. Third American edition, New York, 1823.

Cowley has a vision of a descendant of David who shall rule over the kingdom of Israel. Juno then, plunging to earth, calls up baleful Alecto from the mansions of the dire sisters, and begs her aid. Alecto, infected with Gorgonian poisons, repairs to Latium and, entering the palace, takes possession of Queen Amata's gate. At her the Fury flings from her serpentine locks one of her snakes, and plunges it deep into the bosom of the Queen, so that it may incite her anger against the whole household. The poison of the serpent drives the Queen to rage and madness. After having endeavored in vain to persuade King Latinus to break off the match between Lavinia and Aeneas, the Queen, driven by the poison of the Fury, wanders madly through the town.

This is but the beginning of the Fury's work.

Now begins the episode which furnished the ultimate source for Marini and Cowley.

The baleful goddess is borne on dusky wings to the walls of the bold Rutulian, and at the dead hour of midnight enters the palace where Turnus is enjoying repose. Here Alecto, laying aside her hideous aspect and Fury's limbs, transforms herself into a hag, plows with wrinkles her obscene loathed front, assumes gray hairs, and with a fillet binds on them an olive branch. She becomes Calybe, the aged priestess of Juno's temple, and presents herself to the youth. She addresses Turnus and urges him to overthrow the Tuscan armies and to protect the Latins. But he refuses to believe her, and derides her as 'an old woman oppressed with dotage and void of truth.' Alecto kindles with rage, and as for the youth, while yet the words were in his mouth, a sudden trembling seized upon his limbs; his eyes grew fixed at sight of the hissing snakes and the horrid shape of the Fury; as he hesitates and purposes more to say, she, rolling her fiery eye-balls, repels his words, rears the double snakes in her hair, clanks her whip and tells him who she is, whence she comes. Then she flings a fire-brand at the youth, and deep in his breast fixes the torch smoking with horrid light. Excessive terror disturbs his rest, and sweat, bursting from every pore, completely drenches his bones and his limbs. He raves, and frantic calls for arms. Alecto then wings her flight to where Iulus is pursuing beasts of prey. Mounted upon the high roof of the stall, she sounds the shepherd's signal, and stirs up the forces of Tyrrhus and of Ascanius against each other, so that they join in battle and the earth is covered with the blood of the slain. This done, she reports to Juno the success of her hellish designs, and leaving the high places in this upper world, hastens to the mansions below, disburdening thus both heaven and earth.

To this episode, Cowley refers in his note, and criticises Virgil's method : 'Neither do I more approve in this point of Virgil's method, who in the seventh Aeneid brings Alecto to Turnus at first in the shape of a priestess, but at her leaving of him, makes her take upon her the shape of her own figure of a Fury ; and so speak to him, which might have been done, methinks, as well at first, or indeed better not done at all ; for no person is so improper to persuade man to any undertaking as the Devil without a disguise ; which is why I make him here both come in and go out too in the likeness of Benjamin, who as the first of Saul's progenitors might the most probably seem concerned for his welfare, and the easiliest be believ'd and obey'd.'

It is noticeable that, in the case of Crashaw, the Devil assumes the shape of Joseph, the King's dead brother.

It is a remarkable fact, that though Cowley is always ready to quote from the classic poets, though he never hesitates to give the source of a simile or of a metaphor, if taken from Latin or Greek, he never refers to contemporaries or to preceding English poets. In the first instance, he is doubtless led by a scholarly spirit to give his classic authorities ; in the other case, he may have thought the likeness or source would be obvious.

Among all the ancient poets to whom Cowley refers, Virgil is given the precedence. Everywhere Cowley

5

speaks of him in terms of the highest respect and admiration, as 'My Master,' and 'That Prince of Poets.' One needs only a casual glance at the *Davideis* to see how much Cowley, in his epic, was indebted to Virgil, so that one critic[1] says: 'It is crowded with unblushing plagiarisms.' And the opening line of the *Davideis*, 'I sing the man who Judah's sceptre bore,' leads another critic to remark[2]: 'Even the opening of Virgil's Aeneid has proved irresistible to Cowley, who has miserably paraphrased it in the first line of the Davideis. Embarking with such a determined lack of originality, Cowley was still the school-boy copying closely from his models.'

Cowley, in his note, thus justifies himself: 'The custom of beginning all poems with a proposition of the whole work and an invocation of some God for his assistance to go through with it, is so solemnly and religiously observed by all the ancient poets, that though I could have found out a better way, I should not (I think) have ventured upon it. But there can be, I believe, none better; and that part of the Invocation, if it became a Heathen, is no less necessary for a Christian poet. *A Jove principium, Musae;* and it follows then very naturally, *Jovis omnia plena.* The whole work may reasonably hope to be filled with a Divine Spirit, when it begins with a prayer to be so.' Cowley thus felt the tradition too strong to break away from, as did also Milton later, who began his epic with a proposition and an invocation to the Hebrew Muse.

On the whole, however, it must be confessed that the critic of the North British Review is right when he says that Cowley is 'still the school-boy copying closely from his models.' This may be seen by comparing the opening passage of the *Davideis*:

> I sing the man who Judah's sceptre bore
>
> . . . .
>
> Much danger first, much toil did he sustain,
> Whilst Saul and Hell cross'd his strong fate in vain ;
>
> . . . .

---

[1] Wm. Stebbing. *Some Verdicts of History reviewed.* London, 1887.
[2] *North Brit. Review*, Vol. 6 (1846–1847), p. 398.

> So long her conqu'ror Fortune's flight pursued,
> Till with unwearied virtue he subdu'd
> All home-bred malice and all foreign boasts.

With the familiar:

> Arma virumque cano, Trojae qui primus ab oris
> Italiam, fato profugus, Laviniaque venit
> Litora: multum ille et terris jactatus et alto
> Vi superum, saevae memorem Junonis ob iram,
> Multa quoque et bello passus, dum conderet urbem.

Compare also the opening lines of Tasso's *Jerusalem* and of Voltaire's *Henriade*.

And so, all through the poem, passage after passage might be cited showing the closest following of Virgil. Wherever there is the least exaggeration or a seeming departure from truth, Cowley hastens to strengthen his statement by reference to Virgil. Even in the matter of verse as seen below, Virgil is his authority. On a question of style, too, Cowley has recourse to the Latin poet. At the introduction of the ode, *Davideis*, I, 482, the note in the line explains that there is a seeming want of connection between the ode and the preceding line. For this, reference is had to *Aeneid*, III, 84 ff.; IV, 869 ff., in which appears the common construction of the omission of *inquit* before direct discourse. In the description of the Prophet's College, based on English colleges of his own day,[1] Cowley tells of early books, 'Some drawn on fair

---

[1] Compare the academy in the first scene of *Love's Labor's Lost*, and see Gregor Sarrazin, *William Shakespeare's Lehrjahre, Litterarhistorische Forschungen*, Heft V, 1897, p. 205. Sarrazin cites as a parallel and possible hint for Shakespeare, the academy founded in 1592 by Sir Walter Raleigh. It included in its membership Marlowe, Thomas Kyd, Thomas Harriott, Royden, and Warner. The club, however, developed atheistic tendencies, and the assassination of Marlowe was considered the just judgment of God upon him for his impiety.

Compare also the academy of Charlemagne, in which the Emperor and Court assumed names taken partly from the Bible and partly from the Greek and Roman classics. Alcuin was known as Horace, Eginbart as Calliopus, and the Emperor himself as King David.

From such well-known societies and academies as these, Cowley may have derived some hints for his Prophet's College at Rama.

palm-leaves, with short-liv'd toil' and here the note refers to the Sibyl, *Aeneid*, VI, 74, 'Foliis tantum ne carmina manda.'

The feast of Saul, *Davideis*, II, 358 ff., is celebrated in true Roman style, as also the feast of Moab, *Davideis*, III, 271 ff. 'An hereditary bowl with which they made their libations to their gods and entertained strangers' (III, note 33) was crowned with flowers and passed from hand to hand. The room was hung with tapestry, and the guests at the feast reclined upon beds in Roman fashion (II, note 33). In his note to the second passage, Cowley refers to Virgil's description of the feast with which Queen Dido welcomes Aeneas, *Aeneid*, I, 728. Thus, feasts, battles, and even religious ceremonies are distinctly Roman, Virgilian. In nearly every case, Cowley has frankly pointed out his sources.

When, however, we come to compare Cowley with Virgil in the treatment of the episode discussed above, we find that Cowley does not, after all, take many details from Virgil's account. He owes more to Ovid, Statius, and Claudian, as will be shown below.

In his description of hell, one borrowing from Virgil is of interest, for it was later imitated by Dryden. To justify his epithet, 'unfletcht tempests,' I, 75, Cowley either quotes or refers to Aristotle, Hippocrates, Virgil, Juvenal, and the Bible. He quotes from Virgil the well-known passage concerning the cave of Aeolus, *Aeneid*, I, 52. Cowley's lines are :

> 'Beneath the dens where unfletcht tempests lie,
> And infant winds their tender voices try.'

This is not based upon *Aeneid*, I, 52, but rather upon *Aeneid*, X, 97 :

> ceu flamina prima
> Cum deprensa fremunt sylvis, et caeca volutant
> Murmura, venturos nautis prodentia ventos.

Which Dryden translates in almost the exact words of Cowley :

So winds, when yet unfledg'd in woods they lie,
In whispers first their tender voices try.[1]

Cowley, however, is still closer to Statius :

Illic exhausti posuere cubilia venti. *Thebaid*, I, 37.
Ventus uti primas struit inter nubila vires. *Theb.*, VII, 625.

Marini in his treatment of this episode, *Strage degli Inno-centi*, stanza 61, has taken bodily the figure used to describe Herod's rage, from Virgil's *Aeneid*, VII, 462–466.

[1] Dryden afterwards parodied this couplet in *Mac Flecknoe*, ll. 76, ff.

Where unfledg'd actors learn to laugh and cry,
Where infant punks their tender voices try.

A writer in *Littell's Living Age*, 5th series, vol. 40 (Oct.–Dec. 1882), p. 753, has pointed out later imitations of these lines of Cowley :

Compare Young's *Night Thoughts*, Night IX (Anderson's *British Poets*, p. 125, col. b) :

above the caves
Where infant tempests wait their growing wings,
And tune their tender voices to that roar.

Mrs. Barbauld, *The Invitation*, ll. 83-84 :

Here callow chiefs and embryo statesmen lie,
And unfledg'd poets short excursions try.

In still another passage of his translation Dryden has imitated Cowley. Compare the death of Goliath, *Davideis*, III, 589 :

Down, down, he falls ! and bites in vain the ground,
Blood, brain, and soul crowd mingled through the wound.

A passage based upon *Aeneid*, X, 349 :

Fronte ferit terrum, et crassum vomit ore cruorem,

which is translated by Dryden :

His forehead was the first that struck the ground,
Life-blood and life rush'd mingled through the wound.

Compare also *Aeneid*, IX, 752 :

ingenti concussa est pondere tellus :
Collapsos artus et arma cruenta cerebro.

which Dryden translates :

Down sinks the giant with a thund'ring sound,
His pond'rous limbs oppress the trembling ground,
Blood, brains, and foam, gush from the gaping wound.

IMITATIONS OF THE AENEID, VII, 286 FF. PRECEDING
COWLEY.

In many of the Joseph dramas described by Von Weilen, *Der Agyptische Joseph*, etc., this same episode has been
imitated.

In the Spanish Tragedia, *llamada Josefina*, by Mical de
Cravajal, Placencia, 1546 (von Weilen, p. 13), the poet
introduces in the fourth act, *Invidia, furia infernal*, who
complains that, though everything else lies at her feet,
Jacob and his race resist her. She calls to her assistance
the demons of hell and sends her four daughters, the
Furies, to incite the brothers against Joseph. They successfully accomplish their mission, and Joseph is sold into
captivity.

In Brunner's German drama, or *Biblische Historia*, published at Wittenberg, 1566 (von Weilen, p. 92), appear in
the first scene two devils, Belial and Moloch, who incite
the brothers against Joseph, and later instigate Potiphar's
wife to tempt him (compare Fracastor's *Joseph* below).

Upon the subject of Herod and Mariamne appeared not
long after 1544 a drama entitled *Mariamne* by Lodovico
Dolce.[1] In the second prologue, Pluto, the Prince of
Hell, who has heard of God's plan of salvation for man-
kind, resolves to get possession of Herod's soul. Envy
(Gelosia) appears before Pluto and offers her services.
Pluto praises her faithfulness, but resolves to undertake
the mission himself. The devils do not appear again.

A far more complete and careful treatment of this episode, a close parallel to Cowley, is seen in Jerome Fracastor's *Joseph*, a Latin poem in two books, which appeared
in his *Opera Omnia*, etc., Venise, 1555.

Jerome Fracaster was one of the most celebrated scholars of his time. Born at Verona in 1483, he became Professor of Logic at Padua, at the age of nineteen. He
established his reputation as a poet by the publication of
his *Syphilodis, sive morbi gallici, libri tres, Verone*, 1530, in

---

[1] See Marcus Landau. *Die Dramen von Herodes u. Mariamne, Zeitschrift
für vergleichende Litteraturgeschichte, Neue Folge*, VIII, 183.

which he traces the origin of this loathsome disease syphilis to ancient times. His poem was very popular, and was translated into many languages.

Joseph was the last of his works, and was left unfinished at his death in 1553. It must have been known to Marini, and to Cowley it was made familiar by Joshua Sylvester's translation, entitled *The Maiden's Blush, or Joseph, Mirror of Modestie, Map of Pietie, Maze of Destinie, or rather of Divine Providence. From the Latin of Fracastorius, translated and dedicated to the High Hopefull Charles, Prince of Wales, by Joshua Sylvester*. It was entered upon the Stationers' Register Dec. 6th, 1619. See Grosart's edition of Sylvester, *Chertsey Worthies Library*, 1879, II, 103 ff. Sylvester's translation contains 1799 lines and is written in heroic couplets.

The poem begins with the usual invocation, but there is no picture of hell here as in Cowley and in Crashaw. Pluto, the poet relates, knowing that from Abraham's stock the Saviour of mankind is to spring, becomes perplexed and vexed sore, and therefore, 'he labors and he lays about, with all the engines of his hellish hate, that dear issue to exterminate.' He incites the anger of the brethren against Joseph, so that they cast him into the pit. But the Almighty takes pity upon Joseph and sends down an angel to comfort him.

When Joseph is finally sold, and brought before Potiphar, Iempsar, Potiphar's wife, conceives a guilty passion for the young Egyptian. Pluto, seeing his opportunity, calls forth a cruel Harpy full of wicked wile (the Latin has 'unum servorum'), and commissions him to inflame Iempsar's lust still more, and if possible to 'set Joseph, too, afire.'

> He, glad and ready for the worst of ills,
> With Stygian puddle half a vial fills,
> Blending some bitter sharp-sweet wine withal.
> Then snatching quick one of the snakes that crawl
> About Alecto's grim and ghastly brows,
> Away he hies to Potiphar his hows,
> Within his bosom hiding what he had,
> And formerly just in the form him clad
> Of Iphicle, the lady Iempsar's nurse.

In this disguise he addresses her, encourages her in her desires, and gives her, as a love potion, 'the hellish philter' which excites her passions still further. Clothing himself then as a hag, he hastens to Joseph's chamber, but finds the young man praying and praising God, and is driven off by a heavenly warder with a shining sword. Whereupon, he assumes the form of an owl, and perches upon the roof. Here ends Book I in the Latin. Sylvester prints both books in one.

Iempsar, meanwhile, influenced by the poison, tempts Joseph, but he resists her advances and leaves her. At this the devil upon the roof 'puts off the fowl and re-puts on Nurse Iphicle a space,' enters to Iempsar and encourages her to make a second attempt. This she does, but is again repulsed by Joseph, who tells her the real character of the supposed Iphicle. Upon this the fury, who was hiding behind the door, rushes forth, and seizing one of her snakes, throws it at Joseph, but the heavenly warder again saves him. Unable to hurt him, the snake crawls to Iempsar, creeps into her skirts, gnaws into her very vitals, and infuses his poison into her soul. Furious, she seizes Joseph's cloak, so that he flees in terror. The fiend then incites Iempsar to accuse Joseph of having attempted her honor :—

> All which and more false Iphicle avers
> And aggravates, adjudging him exempt
> From pity, fit to hang for such attempt
> So insolent, so impudent, and whets
> The hearer's hearts ; then close away she gets,
> Unseen and owl-like in a cloud involv'd,
> Her borrowed body into air dissolv'd,
> Descending swift from whence she came, to tell
> Her good ill-service and success in Hell.

In the opening lines, the expression *erat suspectus Jacob* is to be compared with Marini's title *Sospetto d'Herode*.

Here we find a parallelism between Fracastor (or Sylvester) and Cowley, which does not appear in Crashaw. When Joseph is cast into the pit, the Lord looks down with tender compassion upon him, and calling one of his

winged messengers to him, sends him down to comfort
Joseph. Similarly, we find in the *Davideis*, following immediately upon the Devil's successful attempt to incite
Saul against David, a picture of God in Heaven looking
down in pity upon David and sending a herald to comfort
him. This episode is wanting in the *Sospetto*. Cowley
has a long description of Heaven, with the Almighty
surrounded by his angels, evidently based on Statius,
Theb., I, 211 ff. and on Virgil's *Aeneid*, X, 101 ff., to
whom Cowley refers in a note. Otherwise the two passages in Cowley and Sylvester correspond closely.

In Sylvester, the angel's flight is thus described :

> The hill-born nymphs with quav'ring warbles sing
> His happy welcome : caves and rocks do ring
> Redoubled echoes: woods and winds withal
> Whisper about a joyful Madrigal.

While Cowley thus pictures it :

> The jocund spheres began again to play,
> Again each spirit sung Halleluia.

Of the swiftness of the angel's flight, we read in Sylvester :

> And through the *woundless* welkin swifter glides
> Than Zephyrus : or than (when mounted high
> With many turns and tow'ring in the sky)
> The stout Ger-faulcon stoopeth at the Herne
> With sudden souse that many scarce discerne,
> Such was the speed of the celestial bird.

In Cowley :

> Even so
> (But not so swift) the morning glories flow
> At once from the bright sun, and strike the ground :
> So winged lightning the soft air does *wound :*
> Slow time admires and knows not what to call
> The motion, having no account so small.

In Sylvester, the angel then appears to Joseph, comforts him, tells him God is his friend, and reveals to him
the future, with a prophecy of the Saviour who is to spring
from Joseph's stock.

In Cowley, the angel comes to David, comforts him, and prophesies to him the Saviour of mankind, who is to spring from David's stock.

It appears evident, then, that Cowley knew and read the *Maiden's Blush* among the works of Joshua Sylvester. It is not an improbable supposition that Cowley read the original Latin of Fracastorius.

In the *Divine Weeks* of Du Bartas appears still another handling of this same theme (see *The Law*, 3d Part, 3d Day, II Week, ll. 36-120), namely, where Envy incenses Pharaoh to oppress the Israelites. First is given a description of Envy's palace. To her, swift-flying Fame reports the prosperity of Israel. Envy—

> Swoln like a toad, between her bleeding jawes
> Her hissing serpents' wriggling tails she chawes,[1]
> And hasting hence in Isis form she jets.

Disguised thus in the form of the goddess, she appears to the sleeping Pharaoh and urges him to bestir himself, and take arms against the dangers that threaten him. With that she blows into his breast a baneful air, which flows through all his veins and 'makes reason stoop to sence in every part.'

Compare especially Sylvester, ll. 92-93, with the *Davideis*, I, 229-230. See above, p. 34.

In 1587 appeared at Cracow a Latin drama, *Castus Joseph*, by the Polish priest Simon Simonides (Szymono-wicz).[2] This play opens with a long monologue by the Malus Dæmon, who is hostile to the Hebrew race because of the old prophecy, 'pedibus . . . saeviret super caput meum,' so he seeks to ruin Joseph by means of a woman, Potiphar's wife Iempsar. The devils appear, however, only in the opening scene.

---

[1] Compare the *Sospetto*, 'The while his twisted tail he gnaw'd for spite.'

[2] Cited by R. M. Werner in the review of Von Weilen *Der Ägyptische Joseph*, etc., *Zeitschr. für deutsches Altertum*, Vol. 33, pp. 47-48. Werner says the play shows no influence of the western versions. Potiphar's wife is here called Iempsar,—a name, thinks Werner, invented by the poet (foot note, p. 49). But this name at once connects the play with Fracastor's *Joseph*, by which it was doubtless influenced.

Tasso in his *Gerusalemme Liberata* (1575) has made use of this episode from the *Aeneid*. In 1594 Richard Carew published his translation of the first five books of Godfrey of Bulloigne. In 1600 appeared Edward Fairfax's translation, a work far superior in every respect to Carew's, and considered one of the glories of Elizabeth's reign. A second edition was published in 1624.

Book IV opens with a scene in hell. The devil assembles his fiends and sends them forth against the Christians. False Hidraort, the wizard, is employed by Satan to further his evil designs. Hidraort sends his niece Armida to ensnare the Christian knights. The picture of hell is drawn with power and great imagination, and there is no doubt that Cowley consulted this passage in Fairfax's translation. Compare especially the effect of Satan's rage, *Davideis*, I, 147 ff., with Fairfax, Book IV, stanza 8.

In Book VIII, stanza 72, Alecto 'strews wasteful fire' among the Italians, and incites them to revolt. Stanza 74 is borrowed directly from *Aeneid*, VII, 462–466, exactly the same passage which Marini appropriated to describe Herod's rage, *Strage degli Innocenti*, stanza 61 (see above, p. 65).

In Book IX we find the imitation of the episode from Virgil, an almost exact parallel to Cowley.

In the opening stanzas, Alecto disguises herself,

> and semblant bore
> Of one whose age was great, whose looks were grave,
> Whose cheeks were bloodless, and whose locks were hoar.

She appears then at the bed-side of Soliman, and urges him to active efforts against the Christians:

> This said, her poison in his breast she hides,
> And then to *shapeless air* unseen she glides.

Compare p. 56 above, and also

> Straight into *shapeless air* unseen she fell.
> *Davideis*, II, 838.

There are also other passages in which Cowley's indebtedness to Tasso may be traced. Compare the *Invocation* in each, and the following: Description of Gabriel, *Davideis*, II, 793 ff.; Fairfax, Canto, I, stanzas 13 ff.; Canto IX, stanza 59; though here both Tasso and Cowley borrow from the classics, Homer, *Iliad*, XXIV, 339; *Odyssey*, V, 43; Virgil, *Aeneid*, IV, 238; Statius, *Thebaid*, I, 303. Compare also Milton, *Paradise Lost*, V, 246.

Mention must be made of Ben Jonson, *The Poetaster*, in the prologue to which Envy appears with her snakes. Gifford, in a note, compares with the *Davideis*.

When we examine, however, details of this episode in the *Davideis*, we find passages, metaphors and similes taken from almost all Latin and Greek poets.

In his description of heaven, and of the Lord sending an angel to comfort David, Cowley has followed Fracastor, but both Cowley and Fracastor are indebted to Statius, *Thebaid*, I, 192, ff., where Jupiter, in answer to Oedipus's prayer for vengeance, sends Mercury to summon Laius from hell. Compare also *Iliad*, 24; *Aeneid*, IV, 238; X, 101; Tasso, *Gierus. Lib.*, I, 13. The speech of Jehovah, *Davideis*, I, 389, ff., is modelled upon that of Jupiter, *Thebaid*, I, 211 ff. For the whole episode of Envy in disguise inciting Saul to vengeance, compare *Thebaid*, II, 1 ff., where Laius, disguised as Tiresias, appears to Eteocles and urges him to action, a passage referred to by Cowley in a note. From Statius, too, Cowley took not a few features of his description of hell. Compare *Thebaid*, II, 37 with *Davideis*, I, 75. Also the description of Pluto in the infernal regions, *Thebaid*, VIII, and the picture of the furies, Book XI, must have afforded Cowley many suggestions.

From Ovid, Cowley took several features of his description of hell. Compare *Davideis*, I, 71 ff. with *Metamorphoses*, I, 137 ff.; II, 760 ff. (see also Milton, *Paradise Lost*, I, 684). Cowley's description of Envy is largely made up from *Metamorphoses*, II, 760; IV, 431; VIII, 792.

The picture of Satan's rage, *Davideis*, I, 143 ff., is imitated from Claudian, *De Raptu Proserpinae*, I, 83 ff. Compare also Tasso, *Gierus. Lib.*, IV, 8. The speech of Envy to Satan follows closely that of the fury Lachesis to Pluto, *De Raptu Proserpinae*, I, 55 ff., and the speech of Megaera, *In Rufinum*, I, 74 ff. The whole episode in Cowley is to be compared with *In Rufinum*, I, 123 ff.

For the description of hell in the *Davideis* compare also Hesiod's famous description, *Theogony*, ll. 713 ff., a passage to which Cowley refers.

Finally, Cowley's description of heaven is modelled upon his own description of hell; the phraseology corresponds closely.

Hell.

Beneath the silent chambers of the earth,
Where the sun's fruitful beams give metals birth,
Where he the growth of fatal gold doth see,

.   .   .   .

Beneath the dens where unfletcht tempests lie,

.   .   .   .

Beneath the mighty ocean's wealthy caves,
Beneath the eternal fountain of all waves,
Where their vast court the mother waters keep,

.   .   .   .

There is a place deep, wondrous deep below,
Which *genuine night and horror does o'erflow.*
No bound controls the unwearied space, but Hell
Endless as those dire pains which in it dwell.
Here no *dear glimpse of the sun's lovely face*
Strikes through the solid darkness of the place.
No dawning morn does her kind reds display;
One slight weak beam would here be thought the day.

.   .   .   .

Here Lucifer the mighty captive reigns,
Proud midst his woes and tyrant in his chains.

Heaven.

Above the well-set orbs' soft harmony,
Above those petty lamps that gild the night,
There is a place o'erflown with hallowed light,
Where heaven as if it left itself behind,
Is *stretch'd out* far, nor *its own bounds can find.*
Here peaceful flames swell up the sacred place,
Nor can the glory contain itself in th' endless space.

For there no *twilight of the sun's dull ray*
Glimmers upon the pure and native day.
No pale-faced moon does in stol'n beams appear,
Or with dim taper scatter darkness there.

. . . .

Nothing is there to come and nothing past.
But an eternal *now* does always last ;
There sits the Almighty, First of all and End,
Whom nothing but himself can comprehend.

Heaven is thus only the negative of hell, and both descriptions are but lifeless catalogues of details full of childish conceits.

SUMMARY.

After having examined in detail the poems of David preceding Cowley, the conclusion was reached that Cowley received from Du Bartas the suggestion and inspiration of the *Davideis,* and that, in basing his religious epic upon the *Aeneid,* he likewise followed the precedent of the French poet.

For general outline of the treatment, however, Cowley owes more perhaps to Virgil than to any other writer.

The striking verbal correspondence between the *Davideis,* I, 70 ff. and the *Sospetto D'Herode* was discussed at length, and, from the evidence attainable, it was concluded that Cowley in this episode imitated Crashaw, but did not use Marini, Crashaw's original. Further, both Marini and Cowley were indebted to Virgil's *Aeneid,* VII, 286 ff. Other imitations of this same episode from Virgil were examined, and it was concluded that Cowley made use of Sylvester's translation of Fracastor's *Joseph,* and also of Fairfax's *Tasso.* Finally a brief discussion was given of Cowley's indebtedness to the classic poets; namely, in addition to Virgil, Statius, *Thebaid,* Ovid, *Metamorphoses,* Claudian, *In Rufinum* and *De Raptu Proserpinae,* and Hesiod's *Theogony.*

METRE OF THE DAVIDEIS.

THE HEMISTICH.

In note 14 to Book I of the *Davideis*, Cowley attempts to justify his use of the broken line by reference to Virgil : 'Though none of the English poets, nor indeed of the ancient Latin, have imitated Virgil in leaving sometimes half verses (where the Sense seems to invite a man to that Liberty) yet his authority alone is sufficient, especially in a thing that looks so naturally and gracefully, and I am far from their Opinion, who think that Virgil himself intended to have filled up those broken Hemistiques : There are some places in him which I dare almost swear have been made up since his death by the putid Officiousness of some Grammarians.' Then follow quotations from Virgil and Ovid to establish this point. Cowley seems to have imagined that he was introducing a new feature into English poetry, yet Francis Quarles, only a few years before, had made frequent use of the hemistich, and it appears also in Peele's *King David and Fair Bethsabe*, ed. Boyce, London, 1828, I, 279.

In the *Davideis*, the following examples appear :—

5-stressed line—
    O my ill-changed condition ! O my Fate ! I, 141.

4-stressed line—
    Such is the sea, and such was Saul. II, 19.

3-stressed lines—
    Did I lose heaven for this ? I, 142. One hour will do your work. I, 584. By the Great Name 'tis true. II, 380.
    'twill be a smaller gift. III, 895. It did so, and did wonders. IV, 55. Yet such, Sir, was his case. IV, 1047.

2-stressed line—
    And both for God. IV, 676.[1]

[1] Schipper, *Altengl. Metrik*, II, 210, in treating Cowley's use of the broken line, makes a curious slip in quoting examples of *Cowley's* metre from Mrs. A. Behn's and Nahum Tate's translations of the *Book of Plants*.

Cowley's use of the hemistich is often artistic and effective. For instance, Satan, expressing his rage at David's success, suddenly breaks off with,

> O my ill-changed condition ! O my Fate !
> Did I lose heav'n for this? I, 141.

And again the speech of Michel to the pursuers of David is suddenly broken by her tearful utterance,

> One hour will do your work.

Cowley evidently felt the limitations of the rime, and, lacking skill in varying the position of the caesura, tried to gain the same end by a rhetorical device.

Dryden makes frequent and skilful use of the hemistich, yet, in his *Discourse of Epic Poetry* (1697), he objects to Cowley's view of the broken line in Virgil, and inclines to the contrary opinion, namely that the Latin poet intended eventually to fill in the half verses (Malone, III, 585 ff.): 'But there is another thing in which I have presumed to deviate from him and Spenser. They both make hemisticks, or half verses, breaking off in the middle of a line. I confess there are not many such in the Faery Queen ; and even those might be occasioned by his unhappy choice of so long a stanza. Mr. Cowley had found out that no kind of staff is proper for an heroic poem, as being all too lyrical ; yet though he wrote in couplets, where rhyme is freer from constraint, he frequently affects half verses, of which we find not one in Homer, and I think not in any of the Greek poets or the Latin, excepting only Virgil, and there is no question but that he thought he had Virgil's authority for that license. But I am confident our poet never meant to leave him or any other such a precedent. . . . On these considerations, I have shunned hemisticks, not being willing to imitate Virgil to a fault ; like Alexander's courtiers, who affected to hold their necks awry, because he could not help it.' Evidently this applied only to his translation of Virgil, in which he felt that the broken lines did not properly belong, and that thus, in his capacity as translator, he had no right to introduce them ; in his dramas, on the contrary, the hemi-stich is common.

As to the significance of the broken lines in Virgil, scholars to-day are divided in opinion, some holding to Cowley's view and some to Dryden's. Dryden, however, was totally wrong in his conception of Spenser's use of the hemistich in his *Faerie Queene*. There are but two examples to be found : in Book II, canto VIII, l. 500, and in Book III, canto VI, l. 405, in both of which the stanza is clearly defective. In *Colin Clout's Come Home Again*, l. 695, is an odd line, where, however, the corresponding line has evidently been lost. The only undoubted exam-ple in Spenser appears in the *Shepherd's Calendar*, Feb-ruary, l. 238, where Cuddy interrupts Thenot's long speech.

Denham, in his translation of the *Aeneid* (written in 1636, published about twenty years later), had used the hemistich, but as it occurs only in lines corresponding to the Latin, and as it appears in none of his other poems, he doubtless did what Dryden avoided, 'imitated Virgil to a fault.' In Waller, not a single example appears. Early in the next century, Garth, in his translation of the *Meta-morphoses*, still held to Cowley's view of the broken lines in the *Aeneid;* Pope inclined to Dryden's opinion and excluded them from his verse.

The hemistich, however, founded thus by Cowley upon a doubtful conception of Virgil's metre, and established by Dryden through an erroneous idea of Spenser's verse, became a recognized license in English poetry, persisting even to our own day. Keats introduces into his heroic couplets short lines of two and three stresses, which, how-ever, always rime, for example in his *Callidore* (see Schipper, *Altengl. Metrik*, II, 220).

THE TRIPLET.

In the *Davideis*, there is no example of the triplet, but in the *Anacreontics*, written at about the same time, appear a considerable number as follows :

6

I *Love*, ll. 1–3 Kings: things: strings; ll. 12–14 lyre: inspire: desire; ll. 15–17 Kings: things: strings. III *Beauty*, ll. 21–23 express: undress: nakedness. IV *The Duel*, ll. 3–5 enemy: I: defy; ll. 22–24 maintain: vain: remain. V *Age*, ll. 9–11 take: make; stake. IX *The Epicure*, ll. 25–27 crave: have: grave.

Here the lines are tetrameters, and the verse is very free. In his heroic couplets the following examples were noted:

Of Liberty, Grosart, II, 314, ll. 7–9 stay: away: play. *Of Agriculture*, Grosart, II, 324, *Country Mouse*, ll. 15–17 wheat: meat: eat. *Of Myself*, Grosart, II, 341, Martial L, 10, Ep. 47, ll. 3–5 all: call: small. *Prologue to Cutter*, ll. 17–19 by: cry: why. *Epilogue to Cutter*, ll. 11–13 Cavalier: here: were. *Discourse concerning the Government of Oliver Cromwell*, Grosart, II, 307, ll. 23–25 shew: do: slew; ll. 44–46 throne: grown: one.

Cowley occasionally introduces two couplets together, with the same rime. Of these there are three examples in the *Anacreontics*; II *Drinking*, ll. 16–20 high: why: I: why: VII, *Gold*, ll. 17–21 hate: debate: separate: create. IX *The Swallow*, ll. 15–19 pray: away: away: to-day. In the *Davideis* there are two examples: sell: well: Israel: foretell I, 917; dare: there: care: prayer IV, 737. Also in the *Essays*, *Country Mouse*, Grosart, II, 324, ll. 50–54 repel: cell: tell: fell.

These cases seem, however, due to carelessness rather than to design. Thus in all Cowley's poetry there are only fifteen examples of the triplet; in his heroic couplets, only seven. Evidently, therefore, Cowley regarded the triplet as a metrical license. See also Mead's statement[1]: 'Of Pope's predecessors, Cowley and Dryden show most partiality for the triplet' (p. 43). Cowley and Dryden, however, are not to be classed together in their use of the triplet, for in 4000 lines of Dryden (*Absalom and Achitophel*, *Religio Laici*, *Hind and Panther* I–III) appear 200 triplets (Mead).

[1] W. E. Mead. *The Versification of Pope in its Relation to the Seventeenth Century*, Leipzig, 1889.

Of the other poets of this period, Milton never uses the triplet. Waller has only three examples. Denham's *Cooper's Hill* contains none, but there are six in his *Destruction of Troy* (Mead).

Dryden, *Discourse of Epic Poetry*, was the first that attempted to explain the rhetorical and metrical value of triplets, namely, that they ' bound the sense.' According to Dr. Johnson, though ' Dryden did not introduce the triplet, he established it. Dryden seems not to have traced it higher than to Chapman's Homer; but it is to be found in Phaer's Virgil (1558) written in the reign of Mary, and in Hall's *Satires*, published five years before the death of Elizabeth.'

The triplet thus established by Dryden became very popular and was affected by all the poets from Cowley to Wordsworth.

Schipper in his discussion of the triplet, *Altenglische Metrik*, II, 207, has overlooked these examples in Phaer's Virgil spoken of by Dr. Johnson. The earliest instances cited by Schipper are from Joseph Hall's *Satires*, written in heroic couplets, in which there are only four triplets. Book IV, satires 1, 4, 6. Book V, satire 3.

See also H. M. Regel. *Über George Chapman's Homerübersetzung, Englische Studien*, IV, 336. In the *Iliad* Regel finds 36 examples of the triplet; in the *Odyssey* 121. Regel also refers to Phaer's Virgil, in which he says the triplet is not uncommon, (between 175 and 200 examples). ' Im heroischen couplet,' continues Regel, ' finden sie sich beinahe von anfang an fast bei allen dichtern, die in diesem metrum geschrieben haben. Sie sind überhaupt bei den langzeilen seltener als bei den fünffüssigen jamben.' He gives, however, no examples in support of his statement, and indeed the facts do not seem to bear it out, certainly for the early period of the language. No one seems to have pointed out the fact that triplets appear in Middle English verse. Here they are rare in the short line, but more common in the long line. In the short line in *Seven Sages* (Percy Society, vol. 16, l. 337) is one example, *Caton :*

mone: to-don. In Weber's text (*Metrical Romance*, vol. 3, l. 915), one example, *falle: withalle: falle.* In *Vox and Wulf* (Mätzner *Alteng. Sprachproben*, 1, 136, l. 293), one example, *iwisse: blisse: forgeveness.* But in the long line instances are frequent. In Horstmann's *Early South English Legendary* (E. E. T. S., vol. 87), written in the long line, septenaries and alexandrines, examples of triplets are numerous. The long line indeed is just where we should expect to find the triplet first, for here the jingle of the rime would be less noticeable. The appearance of the triplet in the long line of Chapman's Homer and of Phaer's Virgil is to be connected with the not uncommon use of the triplet in the *Early South English Legendary* (1280–1290). The triplet seems, however, to have been of little significance in Middle English verse, just as it was later until Dryden made it popular. But the fact that it appears in Middle English has not yet been observed by metrists.

ALEXANDRINES.

Still another metrical license which Cowley employed for artistic effect, and which, too, he considered an innovation in English poetry, was the introduction into the heroic couplet of the Alexandrine, or long line of twelve syllables. Here again he has recourse to Virgil as his authority (Book I, note 25 of *Davideis*): ' I am sorry it is necessary to admonish the most part of my readers that it is not by Negligence that the verse is so loose, long, and, as it were, vast; it is to paint in the Number the Nature of the thing which it describes, which I would have observed in various other parts of this Poem, that else will pass for very careless Verses: "And overruns the neighb'ring Fields with violent Course"' (*Davideis*, 1, 60). Here follow various other examples of the same kind. 'The thing is,' he continues, 'that the Disposition of words and Numbers should be such as that out of the Order and Sound of them, the things themselves may be represented. This the Greeks were not so accurate as to bind themselves to; neither have our English Poets observed it, for ought I can find. The Latins (qui Musas colunt severiores), sometimes did it, and their Prince, Virgil, always.'

In the *Davideis* there are 25 Alexandrines, as follows: I, 60, 354, 832; II, 611, 718; III, 366, 844, 1035; IV, 79, 92, 143, 189, 303, 325–333, 351, 661, 840, 922.

In the long passage IV, 325–333, God's speech is written in Alexandrines in order to give greater dignity to the language, and so anxious is the poet to gain the desired effect, that he makes the Almighty use the first person plural of majesty. (See Johnson, Life of Cowley.)

Other examples of Alexandrines appear as follows: *On the Death of Mr. Crashaw*, ll. 8, 16, 34, 44, 64, 74. Here again the long lines are used to lend dignity to the language. Verses in the *Discourse Concerning the Government of Oliver Cromwell*, Grosart, II, 307, ll. 20, 54; ibid., II, 308, col. b., l. 14: *Answer to a Copy of Verses sent me to Jersey*, last line, ibid., I, 145a; *Essays, Danger of Procrastination*, ibid., II, 338a, l. 5; II, 339a, l. 12; *Of Myself*, ibid., II, 341a, ll. 28–29. Total 15.

Total number of Alexandrines in his poetry, 35.

The fact that Cowley was the first poet to mingle the Alexandrine with the heroic couplet has already been pointed out by Dr. Johnson, who, however, at the same time, condemned the practice: ' I know not whether he has, in many of these instances, attained the representation or resemblance that he purposes. Verse can only imitate sound and motion. A *boundless* verse, a *headlong* verse, and a verse of *brass*, or of *strong brass*, seem to comprise very incongruous and unsociable ideas. What there is peculiar in the sound of a line expressing loose care, I cannot discover nor why the pine is taller in the alexandrine than in ten syllables.'

Dryden, *Discourse of Epic Poetry*, Malone, III, 522, thus justifies his use of the Alexandrine: 'Spenser has also given me the boldness to make use sometimes of his Alexandrine line, which we call, though improperly, the

Pindarick, because Mr. Cowley has often employed it in his odes. It adds a certain majesty to the verse, when it is used with judgment, and stops the sense from overflowing into another line.'

It is interesting to note that in one instance Cowley closes the triplet with an Alexandrine. In the verses in *Discourse Concerning the Government of Oliver Cromwell*, Grosart, II, 307b, ll. 15–17 :

> The great Jessæan race on Judah's throne,
> 'Till 'twas at last an equal wager grown ;
> Scarce Fate, with much ado, the better got by one.

It was this same trick of verse which Dryden afterwords so much affected, and which, in his *Discourse on Epic Poetry*, Malone, III, 537, he thus justifies : ' When I mentioned the Pindarick line, I should have added that I take another license in my verses, for I frequently make use of triplet rhymes, and for the same reason,—because they bound the sense. And therefore I generally join these two licenses together and make the last line a Pindarick ; for besides the majesty which it gives, it confines the sense within the barriers of these lines, which would languish if lengthened into four. Spenser is my example for both these privileges of English verse,[1] and Chapman has followed him in his translation of Homer. Mr. Cowley has given in to them after both ; and all succeeding writers after him. I regard them now as the Magna Charta of heroick poetry.'

FEMININE RIMES.

In the *Davideis* there is no example of a feminine rime, and it is not common in the other poetry of Cowley. The feminine rime was generally excluded from the heroic couplet by the seventeeth century poets. In Milton, Waller, and Dryden, examples are few. See Mead, pp. 45–46. In the heroic couplets of Cowley there are only nine examples.

---

[1] In the *Shepherd's Calendar* there are six triplets.

In the rest of his poetry there are 57 examples, appearing, for the most part, in the *Pindaric Odes* and *Anacreontics*, where the verse is free.

RUN-ON LINES AND RUN-ON COUPLETS.

On Cowley's use of the heroic couplet, Schipper remarks (II, 210): 'Das *enjambement* bedient er sich neben den gewöhnlichen Licenzen wie Taktumstellung und Wandel der Cäsur, in nicht seltenen Fällen. Reimbrechung kommt nur ganz vereinzelt vor. Auch sind die Reime fast durchgehends stumpf.'

In Cowley's early poems, his use of the heroic couplet is very free, as appears from the following table :

		No. lines.	Run-on lines.	Run-on couplets.	Mid-stopt lines.	Broken rimes.
1632	*Elegy on Death of Lord Carleton*	28	23%	21%	3%	0
1633	*Elegy on Death of Mr. Rd. Clerke*	36	20%	11%	3%	0
1633	*Dream of Elysium*	98	32%	24%	7%	1
1633	*On His Majesty's Return out of Scotland*	54	42%	44%	11%	0
1636	*Elegy on Death of John Littleton*	64	28%	28%	13%	1
1636	*Elegy on Death of Mrs. Ann Whitfield*	36	44%	38%	13%	1

To be compared with this are two humorous poems in which the verse is designedly free :

		No. lines.	Run-on lines.	Run-on couplets.	Mid-stopt lines.	Broken rimes.
1636	*Poetical Revenge*	54	66%	71%	24%	12
1645	*Answer to a Copy of Verses sent me to Jersey*	52	42%	36%	8%	1

Here there is a marked increase in the per cent. of run-on lines, run-on couplets, and mid-stop lines.

In 1637 Cowley entered the University, and from this time forward his verse becomes more correct, as may be seen from the following table :

		No. lines.	Run-on lines.	Run-on couplets	Mid-stopt lines.	Broken rimes.
1639	*To Lord Falkland*	42	21%	23%	0	0
1639	*On the Death of Sir H. Wotton*	28	21%	7%	0	0
1640	*To the Bishop of Lincoln*	56	15%	10%	0	0
1641	*On the death of Sir A. Vandyke*	40	14%	14%	1	0
1650	*To Sir W. Davenant*	40	22%	10%	0	0
1650	*On the Death of Mr. Crashaw*	72	24%	10%	2	2

The following table exhibits his use of the heroic couplet in the *Davideis* :

	No. lines.	Run-on lines.	Run-on couplets.	Mid-stopt lines.	Broken rimes.
Book I	934	19%	13%	6%	1%
" II	838	16%	10%	7%	2%
" III	1034	13%	11%	7%	1%
" IV	1117	23%	19%	10%	2%

Here the verse gradually becomes freer, the increase in mid-stopt lines being especially noticeable. Effective use is made of them in conversation. On the whole, however, the general average of run-on lines, run-on couplets, and mid-stopt lines in the *Davideis* agrees with the average of his other verse at this period.

For the heroic couplets interspersed throughout his prose, of which only the longer pieces are taken (Grosart, II, 307, 323, 324, 325, 326, 333), 612 lines in all, the figures are, run-on lines 18, run-on couplets 19, mid-stopt lines 1.

The results may be tabulated thus :

				Run-on lines.	Run-on couplets.	Mid-stopt lines.
1632–1637	.	.	.	32%	29%	6%
1637–1650	.	.	.	20%	13%	1%
Davideis	.	.	.	18%	14%	1%
1660–1667	.	.	.	18%	19%	1%

It thus appears that Cowley's verse tends to become more 'correct.' The verse of his boyhood, 1632–1637, is free and careless. Upon his entrance to the University a distinct advance is noted ; his verse here had more of his care, and consequently there is a marked decrease in the per cent. of run-on lines and run-on couplets. Since, however, from 1637 on, the per cent. remains almost constant, it is evident that this approach to 'correctness' is due, not to the influence of Waller and of the 'classical school,' but to the natural and gradual improvement of his own verse. In metre, as in almost everything else, Virgil was his authority and court of last resort, and to him Cowley was indebted for every 'improvement' he ventured to introduce into the heroic couplet.